PENGUIN BOOKS
BBC BOOKS

Professor Phil Race is the consultant on the series *Who Learrns Wins* which was first broadcast in February 1995. At the time of writing, he is Professor of Educational Development at the University of Glamorgan and has written and co-authored several other books on learning: *500 Tips for Students*, *500 Tips for Teachers* (with Sally Brown and Carolyn Earlam), *500 Tips for Tutors* (with Sally Brown), *500 Tips for Trainers* (with Brenda Smith) and *How to Win as a Part-time Student* (with Tom Bourner).

Who Learns Wins
Phil Race

PENGUIN BOOKS
BBC BOOKS

To Betty
In admiration of the courage with which you
ascended your final learning curve

Published by the Penguin Group and BBC Enterprises Ltd
Penguin Books Ltd
27 Wrights Lane, London W8 5TZ, England
Penguin Books USA Inc.
375 Hudson Street, New York, New York 10014, USA
Penguin Books Australia Ltd
Ringwood, Victoria, Australia
Penguin Books Canada Ltd
10 Alcorn Avenue, Toronto, Ontario, Canada M4V 3B2
Penguin Books (NZ) Ltd
182–190 Wairau Road, Auckland 10, New Zealand

Penguin Books Ltd, Registered Offices:
Harmondsworth, Middlesex, England

First published 1995
10 9 8 7 6 5 4 3 2 1
Copyright © Phil Race, 1995
All rights reserved

Designed by Ged Lennox
Cartoons by Bill Lisle
Set in Caxton and Franklin Gothic
Printed and bound by Clays Ltd, St Ives plc
Cover printed by Clays Ltd, St Ives plc

This book is published to accompany the BBC Continuing Education television series entitled *Who Learns Wins*, first broadcast in 1995.

Contents

Foreword

The idea of learning something new and different fills me with dread. I am neither academic nor practical. I tend to get very panicky and sweaty when faced with something that I feel may be beyond my capabilities. The older we get the more most of us tend to shy away from new experiences. As adults the prospect of failure is humiliating. Luckily I have the hide of a rhinoceros and am fairly confident that what I can do, I do well.

Having said that, during the discussions for the series I became crashingly aware of how limited I am in the skills department. I began to realize that the list of things I could do amounted to being able to cook spaghetti bolognaise and turn a cartwheel. (Oh yes, I can also pick up a credit card off the floor with my teeth, but that's another story.) Since leaving school in a haze of mediocrity (seven 'O' Levels and two low-grade 'A' Levels), the only thing I had managed to achieve was to pass my driving test – and I was 28 before I managed that.

Now in my thirties, I feel embarrassed by the fact I still can't change a plug, use my computer properly and that I am still vague about things like tyre pressures and oil gauges. Despite being a big girl now, I sometimes tend to perpetuate the myth of 'hopeless girlie', fobbing jobs that I am entirely capable of doing onto my long-suffering partner.

Basically, I'm lazy. I have a problem with my concentration. I tend not to listen properly which usually means things go in one ear and straight out of the other. At school I was easily bored (probably because it was fashionable) and would nod off during lessons only to be awoken by the bell in a pool of dribble.

Being given the opportunity to learn six new things and get paid for it proved to be enormously gratifying. I managed to do things I never thought I could, with varying degrees of success. Perhaps the fact that I was being filmed concentrated my mind. Nevertheless, by the time we'd finished filming, I could order my way round a French restaurant, ski down a hill without breaking anything, place a bet at the races and actually understand the odds, enter a library in order to research a particular subject without fainting in a heap of confusion, ride a motorbike without causing carnage and, best of all, sing with a band.

I probably enjoyed the singing most because for years I have had an emotional block about being tone deaf but despite the fact that when I actually sang with a band in front of a live fee-paying audience it sounded pretty bad, I had such a fantastic time that I really didn't care. Confidence is the key to a lot of all this stuff. I was also lucky enough to be coached by a variety of wonderfully patient teachers who bore with me and encouraged me constantly. And if they were privately thinking, 'This woman is a hopeless case', they never let it show. For that I am eternally grateful.

Jenny Eclair

Jenny Eclair
Comedian and presenter of the series

Acknowledgements

I am very grateful to many friends and colleagues for helping me to develop the ideas in this book, and giving me feedback on my drafts. I particularly thank Sally Brown of the University of Northumbria at Newcastle for a wealth of ideas, and encouragement to keep the book readable and, hopefully, entertaining. I am grateful to Maggy McNorton and Danny Saunders of the University of Glamorgan, who have helped me develop my ideas on how we all learn. I am greatly indebted to Mary Sprent, the producer of the BBC Television series for which this book was first commissioned, for thinking of the themes of most of the chapters in the first place, and giving me very useful feedback on my attempts to capture these themes. I thank Khadija Manjlai of BBC Books for her enthusiastic encouragement and wise comments on my drafts. Most of my life has been spent trying to help people to learn – and all I know I have learned from learners! I thank them all.

Making the most of this book

'Oh, please, no! Don't give me a book about learning. I've done all that. I've been there. I didn't like it! Learning hurt my head. I was glad the day I left school. I don't learn any more. I don't have to now. No-one can force me to learn ever again. Take the book away!'

You're already at 'the university of life'

Lots of people have bad feelings about learning, often left over from long-gone schooldays. Many people have such bad memories about learning that they would not dream of walking into a college, or even buying or borrowing a book to learn from at home. Some people feel that their learning days are over.

In fact, we're learning all the time in our day-to-day lives. We never stop learning. Most of our learning has nothing to do with named subjects such as history, geography, maths or science – yet we're actually still learning bits of all of these all the time. When we find our way to somewhere we haven't been before, there's a bit of geography involved. Whenever we use a map, there's some geography. When we find out something that happened a while ago, we've discovered a new bit of history. When we count our change or add up our score at a game, there's a bit of maths going on. When we put together a recipe or cook a meal, there's quite a bit of chemistry going on. When we make new friends, all sorts of things are going on including some sociology, some psychology, several kinds of communication, and so on. When we do something today that we've never done before – we've learned something more.

So how does it all happen? That's where this book comes in. You can use it to explore things you are already good at, and to work out how you became good at them in the first place. This will help you find

1

What's on the menu – a dozen options

There are many options for you in this book – look at the contents list as a menu. You can pick the courses you like, and you can leave alone any parts you don't like. Use the book to suit yourself. For each of the following 'courses' put a tick in the 'yes please' column, and go to the relevant chapter(s) to find out more.

	Yes please	Go to chapter(s)
1 I'd like to find out that I'm actually far better at learning than I think I am.		**1**
2 I'd like to find out more about how my brain works.		**1**
3 I'd like to find out about new ways of learning things.		**1–9**
4 I'd like to find out how learning things can be fun, and indeed should be fun.		**1–9**
5 I'd like to get rid of bad memories I've got about learning in the past – and to find out that it wasn't my fault anyway.		**1**
6 I'd like to improve on things such as sports and physical fitness.		**3**
7 I'd like to become better at do-it-yourself tasks and at following printed instructions.		**4**
8 I'd like to be better at writing things – letters, reports, or even books.		**5 & 6**
9 I'd like to become better at dealing with numbers.		**7**
10 I'd like to learn enough of a foreign language to get by on my holidays.		**8**
11 I'd like to get a qualification involving me going in for some exams.		**5, 6, 9**
12 I'd like to help my kids or friends become better at learning things.		**1–9**

out more about how you think and about how you learn and, in turn, will help you to become better at learning new things. More importantly, you'll become interested in learning things, because learning will be far more fun than you might have imagined possible.

There's another important benefit when you find out more about how you learn; your confidence increases a lot. In fact, think of people you know who have strong self-confidence – they are usually the sort of people who always seem to be learning new skills.

You've lived all your life at the 'university of life'. We all learn most of what we know and do at this 'university' – in other words in our day-to-day lives, our normal jobs, our normal run of activities such as shopping, cooking, caring, and being with other people. We also learn all sorts of skills linked to our hobbies, pastimes and interests. There are no entrance exams, no age limits, no closing times, no restrictions on what we can try to learn – all subjects are available. Even if you spend some years at an institution of learning such as a college or university, by far the majority of your learning will be with the 'university of life'.

Please don't read this book!

This isn't the sort of book to start reading at page 1 and carry on straight through to the end. Look at the menu on the facing page to find out what the book contains, go to whichever parts interest you most and look at them in any order. However, I suggest that you do work through Chapter 1 before doing anything else, as this is the chapter that is intended to get you thinking about how you yourself learn best – and you can then apply what you find out about yourself to each or any of the topics in the other chapters.

Throughout this book there are quizzes and exercises for you to have a go at. You've already met one of these – the 'menu' I invited you to make choices from. When you have a go at something, I won't leave you high and dry. I have included detailed replies or discussions of the tasks that I ask you to do as you use this book. To get the best out of the book, try not to cheat! In other words, when there's a question or an exercise, have a go at it without looking ahead at the comments which follow it. This gives you the chance to compare your ideas with mine when you read the discussion sections following exercises and questions.

How's your learning? Quiz

You may like to use these two pages to decide how you feel about various kinds of learning before you start using this book, then come back and see where your feelings have got better after trying out ideas in this book.

For each of the statements below, decide how much like you it is, and tick the appropriate column opposite.	This is very like me	This is quite like me	This is not really like me	This is not at all like me
1 When I learn something, I tend to remember it for a very long time.		✓		
2 I find it helpful to get other people's comments on things I do – this helps me learn.		✓		
3 I only learn something when I really want to learn it – the pressure has to come from inside me.	✓			
4 I learn best when other people are putting me under pressure to learn it.			✓	
5 I'm good at exams, and don't worry about them at all.			✓	
6 I have difficulty in getting myself started at learning – I tend to put off starting for ages.	✓			
7 I've got plenty of time to devote to learning new skills.		✓		
8 I've got a real block about maths and sums – I hate them, and can't do them.				✓
9 I enjoy following instructions for practical tasks, such as putting together a self-assembly piece of furniture.	✓			
10 I find it relatively easy to learn enough of a foreign language to get by on holidays.			✓	
11 I'm quick to learn physical activities, such as sports, athletics, and so on.		✓		
12 I'm good at artistic activities such as sketching, drawing and painting.				✓
13 My memory keeps letting me down in everyday matters, let alone when I try to learn something new.			✓	
14 I like being taught. I find it most valuable to have teachers helping me to learn.		✓		

For each of the statements below, decide how much like you it is, and tick the appropriate column opposite.	This is very like me	This is quite like me	This is not really like me	This is not at all like me
15 I prefer learning from books and study-packs, rather than being taught.				✓
16 I'm good at sorting out the important matters from the background things, when it comes to deciding exactly what to try to remember.		✓		
17 I don't think I'm any good at learning – I've often been told so in the past.				✓
18 I've often been told that I haven't really answered the question.				✓
19 When I'm learning something, I prefer to shut myself away in a quiet, private place, and get on with it by myself.		✓		
20 I'm good at making summary notes, containing the important matters that I intend to learn.	✓			
21 My reason for learning is to prove to other people that I can do it.			✓	
22 My reason for learning is to get qualifi-cations I need to be able to do the job I want to do.		✓		
23 My reason for learning is to prove to myself that I can do it.		✓		
24 My reason for learning is that I'm required to do it for my job.		✓		
25 I haven't got any reasons for learning, why should I bother?				✓
26 I'm alright at learning, but tests and exams make me go all to pieces.			✓	
27 I've tried learning many times in my life, but have always come out as a failure!				✓
28 I remember all sorts of useless infor-mation, but can never seem to get a grip on what I need to learn.		✓		
29 Learning is something that's done in schools or colleges; I haven't the chance to go to these places to learn now.			✓	
30 I don't need to learn any more – I'm quite happy as I am.				✓

Good news about the thirty statements!

Please read through these comments on the thirty statements you've been rating yourself for.

1   Don't worry if you think you haven't got one. Memory can be improved a lot, but successful learning is not as dependent on memory as most people think. Later in this book we explore how learning actually takes place.

2   As we'll see later, getting feedback from other people is a very valuable part of successful learning. Take the view that 'there's no such thing as criticism, just feedback'.

3   The more reasons we have for learning something, the more likely we are to succeed, but the 'want' must also be there.

4   It's possible you'll come to resent this pressure. It's best if you yourself want to learn, even when you also have pressure on you from other people. Work out 'what's in it for *me?*'

5   Your learning skills aren't dependent on exam performance but, if you're good at exams, you've got an obvious advantage when it comes to *proving* that your learning has been successful.

6   It's human nature to put off difficult tasks. The good news is that difficulty in getting started can be completely cured! We'll explore some ways of curing this later in the book.

7   In fact, how much time you've got does not really matter nearly as much as you might think. You know the saying 'if you want a job done well, give it to a busy person'. Obviously plenty of time is a luxury – but by no means an essential to successful learning.

8   Many people have a block about maths and sums – a hangover from their schooldays. We'll look at ways of getting rid of such blocks later in this book.

9   It is the sort of process that shows a healthy approach to learning by 'trial and error', and also involves feedback – checking it out

every now and then to see if the job is going sensibly.

10 Learning a language involves all the important natural stages involved in learning in general, and is very good practice.

11 Learning sports involves many of the same processes as learning other skills in our lives. We'll analyze all this in more detail later.

12 If you've already become skilled at these, your skills at learning in general are already well-developed. We'll follow this up in a later chapter in this book.

13 We'll explore a lot more about ways of making your memory work better for you.

14 Good teachers are very useful in amplifying the desire to learn, but we've got to do the learning ourselves – they can't do it for us.

15 In fact, most real learning happens without teachers! The knowledge you gain from printed materials is every bit as real as any learning you did in classrooms.

16 This is a really important skill. It's got a lot to do with being *seen* to be successful at learning. We'll have a look at this later.

17 Forget what anyone has ever told you about your learning abilities in the past. Live in the present now, and work towards a future where learning is successful and fun.

18 Later in this book we'll look at how you can practise answering questions until you're perfect on this count.

19 In real life the chance of finding a quiet, private place is not very good. It's much better to be able to do *some* of your learning wherever you happen to be – in noisy offices, buses, trains, work-shops, absolutely anywhere. Later in this book we look at ideas about learning in 'odd places'.

20 This overlaps with Statement 16 that we've already explored.

21 Not the best reason but powerful for providing a strong 'want' to learn.

22 Again, this relates to the 'want' to learn. Your determination will help to keep you going when you come across the difficult parts in what you are trying to learn.

23 It can be a strong factor in your 'want' to learn but who is going to notice if you later decide you're not so keen to do it after all? In that respect, reasons for learning that involve other people are more likely to see you through the tough parts.

24 The advantage is that other people are going to be interested in whether your learning is successful – so you haven't really the option to bottle out when you come to a particularly difficult bit.

25 If you really can't see any reason for doing some learning, you're not going to last long if you come across any obstacles. This book should give you some additional ideas about *why* you should be doing some learning, if you're in any doubt at the moment.

26 To get due credit for your learning you've got to *show* that you *know*. Don't worry, though, in this book we'll include plenty of down-to-earth advice on how best you can tackle tests and exams.

27 This may be due to the circumstances under which you were trying to learn. This book can help you ensure that in your future learning, you know a lot more about how learning actually happens, and how to prove that your learning has been successful.

28 This book should help you a lot in that vital business of sorting out which areas to get a good grip on.

29 Learning can happen absolutely anywhere. Wherever you are with this book is a place where you can be learning very successfully.

30 If this is 'very like you', I don't think you'd be reading this book, particularly at the end of my responses to this quiz! However old we become, we still learn. We have new skills we need to learn.

1

Monkey business

Monkey see, monkey do

Our relatives from the past are believed to have originated from the monkey family. Actually, some of my relatives still think I am, they tell me! Humankind has sometimes been called 'clever monkeys'. In fact, there's not a lot of difference biologically – our bodies work in similar ways to monkeys' bodies, we have a lot of the same parts. Monkeys are quite good at learning. They learn by copying, watching, trying things out, seeing what works (and what gives them some food as a reward). They also learn by seeing what doesn't work, or finding out what hurts them if they try it. We do all these too, and learn in the process.

Probably the only important difference between monkeys and ourselves is that we can actually think about how we learn. We can think about how we think. We can think about how we think we think. We can think about how we think we think we think – and then we can decide to take something for the headache that gives us. There, we're at least one up on monkeys. Of course, it could be the other way round – they could be thinking about how they think they think they think *without* getting headaches. I don't think so though (and I haven't seen a monkey reading this book yet).

So what *is* this thing called 'learning'?

Go on, look 'learning' up in a dictionary. My own personal definition of 'learning' is rather simpler than you'll find in most dictionaries, and is simply: 'becoming able to do something you couldn't do a little earlier'. The 'something' can be all sorts of things, including:

- learning a few more words of a foreign language
- becoming able to putt the shot a few inches further than yesterday
- finding out how to connect up a new video machine
- seeing how to work out how much food costs you in an average week
- becoming able to make a really good Yorkshire pudding (I can do this myself)
- finding out how to put eardrops into the dog's ears to cure an infection

The list is endless. We're learning all the time. We never really stop. We even learn things when we're asleep – for example we can often remember dreams that we hadn't even imagined yesterday – so we must have learned something.

But don't we forget almost everything we learn?

Yes and no. It's never *entirely* forgotten. Suppose you learn something today, then forget it (or think you've forgotten it). Next time you come across it again, it will 'ring a bell', however vaguely, and you'll be that tiny bit less likely to forget it quickly again. By the forty-second time you've re-learned something, you'll be unlikely to forget it ever again. When we say we've forgotten something, what we really mean is that we can't quite manage to remember it at the moment. We'll probably remember it again sometime later, maybe days – even years later. It's usually still in our minds, but not necessarily near the surface of our thinking. Rather than say, 'I can't remember', I prefer to say, 'sorry, but it's in my "forgettery" just now!' In other words, I'll get it back sooner or later.

In a book about learning, one of the main aims is to make learning rather less haphazard than it is naturally. In other ways, what we need to do is to find out more about how it all works. Then we're more and more in charge of our learning.

So how do we *really* learn?

This is where you come in. During this chapter I'm going to ask you four questions about things you've learned in the past, to help you to work out how your own learning happens best. Please don't look ahead at the comments I've made after the questions until you've had a go yourself. Try Question 1 now – jot down a few words in answer to it. The question is in two parts. Try both.

Question 1

(a) Think of something you're good at – something you know you do well. It doesn't matter what it is – sport, hobby, interest, specialist topic, anything at all. Jot down what it is.

(b) Now, still thinking of that particular thing you're good at, jot down a few words about *how you became good at it.*

Discussion of Question 1

You're not reading this before you've jotted down your own answers to Question 1, are you?

It does not matter what you put for part (a): other people have put down everything under the sun for this part of the question. Answers have included cake-making, ballet-dancing, sex, embroidery, driving, carpentry, using computers, running a marathon, finding a bargain in the sales – you name it (well, you did, didn't you?).

The interesting thing is that the answers to part (b) are surprisingly similar. Typical answers to part (b) are:

- by doing it
- by having a go at it
- practice, and more practice
- by trial and error
- by learning from my mistakes

In short, people become good at things by *doing* them. We don't become good at things just by reading about them. Nor do we become good at things by listening to experts telling us about them. The only way we develop our skills is by having a go ourselves – by putting ideas into practice, and testing them out for ourselves.

See what this means? The best books in the world aren't enough to help us become good at things. In other words, we don't learn much just from books, unless at the same time we're having a go ourselves at using the ideas in the books. That's the main reason that this book contains lots of things for you to try out for yourself. It's not a book just to be read.

Make more mistakes!

Notice one more thing about becoming good at things; it's perfectly alright to learn from one's mistakes. In some ways, this is one of the best ways of learning – as long as the mistakes are not serious. (We would not like airline pilots to learn by their mistakes too much – or doctors – though they probably still do to some extent!) One of the problems many of us had in the early days of our education was that 'mistakes' were often treated as 'bad'. If we positively decide that each mistake is an opportunity to learn something useful, the situation becomes a whole lot better.

So how do I set about *deliberately* learning something new?

Exactly the same way as we've been discussing. We can't use a little switch to turn our brains on to do some studying. It's as simple as we saw above – we learn:

- by doing it
- by having a go at it
- by practice, and more practice
- by trial and error
- by learning from our mistakes

Feeling our way

Another big difference between human beings and monkeys is that we have feelings, and we can *think* about our feelings and express them. We have feelings about all sorts of things. We're lean, mean, feeling machines? Well, I'm not lean (I gave up trying to be this years ago!), and hope I'm not mean, but I feel monkeys no doubt have feelings too – we can tell when they're feeling happy or sad, or playful or relaxed. But monkeys aren't known for describing their feelings.

Probably the most important dimensions of our lives are our feelings. A common greeting is 'how are you feeling?' – especially if we've not been feeling too good for one reason or another. Often, our lives are completely taken over by our feelings – falling in love, grieving at the loss of a friend or loved one, and so on. Even the smallest things in our lives are associated with feelings of one kind or another. Whenever we learn something (or don't manage to learn something) we've got some feelings about it.

Let's move on to Question 2 now. This time we're going to explore *positive* feelings – and how you in particular get to have positive feelings.

Question 2

(a) Think of something about yourself that you *feel good about*. In other words, something about yourself that you have a sense of pride in – something that 'gives you a bit of a glow'. Jot it down now – don't be modest!

(b) (This is the hard bit of Question 2.) Try to work out your justifica-tion for feeling good about what you wrote for part (a). In other words, upon what *evidence* is your positive feeling based? Jot this down now.

Discussion of Question 2

Again, it does not really matter what you put for part (a). Typical answers include honesty, good-nature, good-humour, a caring person-ality, determination, patience, compassion; there are hundreds more things you may have chosen.

Again, however, whatever you put for part (a), it's probable that your answer to part (b) will be similar to one or more of the following:

- other people's reactions
- comments from other people
- because people come to me for help
- the expressions on people's faces
- people thank me for it
- people give me compliments about it
- seeing the results for myself

In short, to feel good about something, most of us need *other people's comments or reactions*.

Feedback and Feelings

'Feedback' is a word which means the same thing as comments and reactions from other people. We all need to find out how we're doing – we need feedback. When we get other people's reactions, we may swell with pride if they were positive reactions. Even when they are negative reactions, feedback is always useful. When we get negative reactions from other people, we can adjust what we do to try to gain a more positive reaction next time.

Think back to what you chose as the thing you feel good about. Whatever it was, it was the result of a great deal of learning. And see how much better we feel about learning things when we feel good about the results. Feelings and learning are inseparable. Whatever we learn, we feel something about it. If we don't feel much at all, we're probably not going to put much energy into the learning. If we actually feel quite negative about something we're learning, we'll probably make all sorts of excuses to stay well away from learning at all. If we feel good about what we're trying to learn, we'll give it our best shot – what's more natural?

To sum up so far, there are two important ingredients for successful learning:

- learning by doing, practising, having a go, including making mistakes
- positive feelings, usually based on other people's reactions to what we do

We've discovered both of these points by thinking of things we do well, and the positive feelings we have about them. Next, we'll look at the other side of the coin – what can we find out by thinking back to bad learning experiences?

Feelings and failings

This time we're going to think of things that went wrong. This is more sinister than useful mistakes we made and learnt from. We're now looking at unsuccessful learning experiences. We're thinking of things we tried to do and did not manage to achieve. This includes things we tried, where we felt we were being looked at as being silly, or dense, or inadequate. We're considering nightmares from the past. We're seeing

" I think Lowetta was more after a 'Darling, you were fabulous!' than a 'Cut! Cut! Cut! That was atrocious. Do it again!'"

what we can learn from our nightmares that may help our best dreams come true.

'Failure' is a dreadful word really. If you look at it logically, a 'failure' is just something you have not yet succeeded at. People fail driving tests every day, and often get very negative feelings at the time about their failures. Sooner or later, the vast majority of people who really want to drive, pass their test. They only have to pass once (at least that's how the law is at present – maybe it should be changed – you'd want to change it if you saw my driving!). And once we've passed – hardly any of us think any more of any times when we failed.

If, when learning something, you've never had anything go wrong in your life, you need not have a go at Question 3. If all of your learning has been successful and productive, you're off the hook for this question – just sit with your arms folded and read the comments that follow the question. (However, I have said this to thousands of people so far, and none have folded their arms.)

Question 3
(a) Think of a learning experience that went wrong – something you didn't end up doing well. Jot down what it was.
(b) As honestly as you can, jot down a few words about *why* it went wrong. Whose fault was it? What happened?

Discussion of Question 3

Actually there are all sorts of answers to both parts of question 3. Whatever you put is right for you. It's surprising how many people mention 'maths' for part (a)! And in part (b) many people write down the names of their maths teachers! That's honest, at least.

Your own answer to part (b) may well have included one or more of the following:

- I didn't want to learn it in the first place
- I couldn't see the point of learning it
- I didn't understand it, I could not make sense of it
- I didn't have the chance to work out what it really meant
- I got bad comments from teachers – this put me right off
- I felt as if I had been made to look silly
- I felt tense and under pressure
- I didn't do enough practice, and did not learn it well enough
- I was too nervous to learn it properly or do it well
- I was afraid of making mistakes

Two concepts that we've already met come out of such answers, and there are two new ones as well.

Those we've already met are the need for learning, 'by doing', with plenty of practice, and with 'learning by mistakes' being seen as alright. The second one is to do with feelings again. If we feel afraid, nervous, or that we're being made to look silly, no wonder our learning is not successful. Negative feelings like these can be very damaging – and are likely to stop us from learning.

Two new factors come out of answers such as those listed above.

Wanting to learn

It's really important to *want to learn* in the first place. If we don't really want to learn something, it's not surprising that we're unlikely to be successful at learning it. If we can't see the point of learning it in the first place, we're hardly likely to really *want to learn* it, and again, we'll probably not succeed. However, all need not be lost. Later in this chapter we'll explore alternatives which can play the same part as a healthy 'want' to learn.

10

TIPS AND WRINKLES | on dealing with failure

1 When you've failed to achieve something, remind yourself that it's not the case that you yourself are a failure – it's just that on that particular occasion you did not quite manage to do one particular thing (or a few things simultaneously).

2 Remind yourself that the word failure means nothing more than 'not having succeeded yet'. Most things that people 'fail' at, they pass sooner or later (ask any driving instructor!).

3 When you don't quite succeed at something, use it as an opportunity to work out the likely causes, so you can bear them in mind next time you try.

4 Remind yourself that many of the greatest people were considered 'failures' at one time or another: Einstein, Churchill, Beethoven, for example. Be glad to be in such company.

5 Don't forget that there's always another chance – and as many chances as you need.

6 Remember that past failures are immediately forgotten just after you succeed!

7 If a thing is really worth doing, it's worth failing at, at first. Otherwise, anyone could do it.

8 Everyone who really wants to do something succeeds at it sooner or later – keep focusing on your want to succeed.

9 A 'failure' is often a really useful (if painful at the time) learning opportunity – use such occasions to make sense of what you're trying to do, and your reasons for trying.

10 Keep reminding yourself of your successes. Display them where you see them every day (cups, trophies, photographs, paintings, certificates – anything you're proud of).

Making sense of it all – 'digesting it'

We need the chance to *make sense* of what we learn. We need to begin to understand it. Probably the best word we can think of for this 'making sense' step is *digesting*. In a way, it's much like digesting our food – taking on board what's good for us from what we've eaten – and beginning the process of discarding what we don't need. We get rid of the 'roughage' sooner or later. Learning is quite similar. When we learn something new, we need to sort out which parts are important enough to retain and store. We also need to sort out which parts are not important enough to be stored – and discard them.

How we're ahead of the monkeys

From those three questions – and your own answers to them – we've now helped to pin down four important parts of the way you and I learn:

- wanting to learn, seeing what the point of it all is (monkeys can't do this);
- learning by doing, practising, having a go, including making mistakes; (monkeys can do this – and probably worry less about their mistakes than we do – in this they may be ahead of us);
- positive feelings, usually based on other people's reactions to what we do; (monkeys probably have positive feelings when they're rewarded or praised, but are hardly likely to take as much notice of their feelings as we ourselves do);
- 'making sense' of what we learn – 'digesting' it, to gain understanding; (here again we're doing something that monkeys can't do to any significant extent).

That's it! It's as straightforward as that. These four ingredients are linked to all kinds of successful learning in one way or another. There is no magic way to learn successfully – it's all a combination of common sense and human nature. This should not surprise us – we're human beings, and learning is to do with having a better understanding of common sense.

In some books about how we learn, you'll find detailed models, using words like 'active experimentation, concrete experience, reflective observation, abstract conceptualization, intrinsic motivation, extrinsic motivation, holistic approaches, serial approaches'. All in all, these terms mean very much the same as the four ingredients we identified (in short, 'wanting, doing, feedback, and digesting').

We'll come back to the importance of those four essential ingredients of successful learning throughout this book. Let's summarize our exploration of how we learn by taking one more look at them:

- *wanting to learn:* seeing what the point of it all is
- *learning by doing:* practising, having a go, including making mistakes
- *positive feelings:* usually based on other people's reactions to what we do
- *'making sense':* 'digesting' what we learn, to gain understanding

The beauty of these is that once we are aware of the way we learn naturally, we can periodically give any of these steps a deliberate boost. We can remind ourselves why we want to learn in the first place.

We can deliberately give ourselves a bit of extra practice. We can choose to try out something to see if it works, and be prepared to look at any mistakes we make as learning opportunities. We can accept the usefulness of positive feelings, and seek feedback from other people to help us feel positive. And we can slow down and 'tread water' while we take that extra little bit of time to make sense of something we've just learned.

Needs must …

In this chapter, we've looked in some detail at the importance of wanting to learn. But what happens if we don't want to learn something? Are we doomed to be unsuccessful? Is it worth trying?

In fact, we've all managed to learn things that we did not want to learn. Quite often, after we've learned them we're quite pleased with ourselves and glad that we did this learning. Let me ask you one more question about your own learning.

Question 4
(a) Think of something you learned successfully, but that at the time you definitely did not want to learn – something that you're now glad you learned. Jot it down.

(b) Now look back and work out what 'kept you at it' till you succeeded? Jot down your 'driving forces'.

Discussion of Question 4

There are many reasons why people learn things they did not really want to – and succeed. Typical answers to part (b) of Question 4 are as follows:

- because I needed to be able to do it as part of my job
- to get promoted, I needed to have it
- people were depending on me, so I needed to learn it
- no-one else was there to do it, so I needed to do it myself

The word in common is *needed*. When we *need* to learn something, we usually manage it. That's how our species survives. The expression, 'needs must when the devil drives' has been around for a long time. In a way, a *need* may not be such a pleasant 'driver' of our learning than a *want*, but the end results can be identical – success. Perhaps the real magic is being able to turn your needs into your wants. If you can do this, your learning will always be well driven.

Now that we've sorted out a lot about how we learn, finally, to end this first chapter, I'd like you to start thinking about *when* and *where* we learn.

Home and away

Places ...

I've already hinted at the fact that most of our learning happens as part of our ordinary home lives, working lives and social lives. We've already looked at how it happens, and it's worth reminding ourselves of when and where it happens.

The short answer is 'all the time and everywhere'. This of course means that we're a little bit more like monkeys than we may have wished to think. Monkeys don't think that a classroom or a library is a place where special learning happens – monkeys will learn (to the best of their ability) anywhere at all. So do we!

We, however, do have certain special learning environments. These can include places such as:

- school classrooms
- college lecture rooms
- laboratories
- workshops
- studios
- training centres
- a table set aside at home for studying
- libraries

... and people

Monkeys probably regard one human being in very much the same way as any other human being. They may get to know particular human beings better than others, but, apart from 'friendship attachments', probably don't think of them as particularly different from others of our species.

We, however, see people rather differently, especially if we're learning from them, or even learning with them. Here are some of the categories that we tend to divide our fellow human beings into when we're learning.

- teachers
- lecturers
- trainers
- supervisors
- managers
- colleagues
- classmates
- partners
- friends

Other people are often very important in our learning. We gain information from them. They explain things to us, helping us to make sense of them. We get feedback from them, helping us to develop our feelings about what we're learning. They often inspire us to want to learn in the first place.

... and things!

We do a lot of our learning from 'things'. These include:

- books
- learning packages
- newspapers and magazines
- television sets and videotapes

10
TIPS AND WRINKLES | on using interactive technology

1 You're extremely unlikely to break it (unless you drop it from a great height). Don't be afraid of things like computers.

2 The worst thing that can happen is that you'll lose some information. Most systems will ask you 'do you really want to lose this?' in one way or another. Even if you do lose information, you can often load it back again (or have it done for you).

3 Stop and have another look at things. Usually, when working with computers you'll be doing so on your own, so no-one need know how many times you look back at something as you gradually make sense of it.

4 Work at your own pace. When you understand everything you see on the screen, push ahead quite quickly. Slow down when you need to think harder about material that's new to you.

5 Find 'a person who knows'. Sometimes with computers it can take ages to work something out for oneself, when a few tips from someone familiar with the system can save hours of your time.

6 When you're learning from a computer-based package, spend a little extra time making brief notes of your own on paper, so you can refresh your memory later.

7 If you're using a word processing system to write lengthy pieces, remember to save your work every few minutes. (Everyone loses two hours of work once when the power goes off, or the computer crashes, or the dog jumps on the machine ...)

8 When you don't understand something, or don't know what to do, write down a question or two, so that next time you're with someone who does know, you can remember what to ask.

9 Remember that you're in charge of the machine – not the other way round! You can always switch it off if you don't like what it does.

10 Capitalize on learning by making mistakes. A computer won't be offended however many mistakes you make. It won't even know.

- computer-based learning packages
- records, compact discs, and audiotapes
- machines and instruments

Learning from the small screen

We learn a great deal from our television sets. Have you noticed just how much people around you remember about the latest episode of their favourite 'soap', documentaries or news programmes with an element of human interest? Yet we are conditioned to forget quite quickly most of the things we see and hear on our television sets. After all, there's not much point remembering what the weather forecast was for a week ago last Thursday. And just imagine how depressed we'd become if we learned the content of every news broadcast – especially if it's all bad news.

Computer-based learning packages

Since we are positively conditioned to forget most of what we see on our television screens, what happens when we start to learn from computer-based learning packages? We're no longer meant to forget most of what we see on the screen.

The up-and-coming generation love computers. People don't need to know a lot about how computers work these days. Most children and teenagers spend a lot of time, and have a lot of fun, with computer games. There may not be a lot of significant learning directly associated with these games, but there's a lot of very useful indirect learning. For a start, such people aren't afraid of computers any more. They don't for a moment imagine that they may press 'the wrong key' and blow the machine to eternity! Furthermore, playing with computer packages encourages people to learn by trial and error – as we've seen, an entirely human way of learning.

Trial and error with a computer has the advantage of privacy – when we make a silly mistake no-one but us knows about it.

In fact, the best computer-based learning packages have already taken into account all the ideas we've been sharing about how people learn. For a start, good packages are interesting and fun – they help us *want* to learn from them.

Furthermore, computer-based learning packages are very much *learning by doing* and, until we've made a decision, pressed a key, or typed in an answer, we aren't allowed to go further. So far so good. It gets better! With a good computer-based learning package, as soon as we've done something, we get *feedback*. We very quickly find out whether the decision we made was correct. More importantly, the best packages tell us at once *why we were wrong*, if we didn't make the correct decision.

With a computer-based learning package, we can have another try tomorrow, or next week or next month – this helps us to make sense of what we've been learning and refresh our minds.

Computer study-stations are increasingly found in schools, libraries, and training centres. The quality of such learning packages is heading quickly towards a level of excellence. With CD-ROM, for example, come all the advantages of real sound (including human voices with all the possibilities of tone-of-voice, emphasis, warmth and credibility that they bring). The colours and graphics can be captivating in their own right, further enhancing the 'want' to learn more.

Many people (particularly young people, but including many relative 'oldies' like myself!) actually *play* with computers, and regard fiddling about with keyboards as fun. The whole feeling of sitting at a computer terminal becomes one associated with pleasure, relaxation, fun, adventure, safety, stimulation, and *control*. People sitting at keyboards are in charge. They are making the decisions. It does not matter

when they make a wrong decision – the computer is already programmed to advise them what to do about this.

All this means that the whole medium of computer-based learning is closely related to the 'fun' dimension of many people's experience with computer systems. It isn't 'work' to go and spend half-an-hour with a computer – it's fun. In my opinion, we're just seeing the start of an explosion of computer-based learning.

But what about learning from television programmes?

Television can have all the impact of moving images, facial expression, close-up shots, and so on. However, a television programme can't stop and give you feedback on what you're thinking at a given moment. And as we've noticed, we're conditioned to forget most of what we see on television quite quickly. Television programmes can play a vital and unique part in our learning – they can help us *change our minds*. In other words, a television programme can completely alter the way we look at something – it can help us change or develop our entire attitude to a theme, subject or issue.

The television series linked with this book is in this category. The producers and contributors to the television programmes bring a vast range of skills and experience to bear on helping us to think again about how we learn. This book can be carried around as a portable extension of the re-thinking that the television programmes helped us to do.

But now we've got videos

We can now capture and save our own television programmes. This is very handy for recording *Match of the Day* when we're out, or for recording films or serial episodes to watch at a later date. But we usually see such recordings once, and wipe the tape. However, we can decide to keep our recordings, and (for example) a series of short programmes about how people learn is likely to be well worth looking at several times over a period of time.

Have you noticed what happens when you see 'a repeat'? After the 'I've seen this already' reaction, we often start noticing all sorts of things that we just did not see during our first viewing. And we continue to notice even more if we have yet another look at the programme. This is all part of the way we learn; what we are doing is 'digesting' or making sense of what we are learning. In short, probably the best way to use television programmes as a learning aid is to record

10

TIPS AND WRINKLES

on keeping up your morale – maintaining your 'want' to learn

1 Remind yourself of the benefits that will accompany your successful learning. Keep in mind 'what's in it for me?'

2 Remember that anything important takes time, and often comes gradually.

3 Don't let mistakes or setbacks put you off – regard them as useful learning experiences.

4 When you come across an obstacle in your pathway of learning, don't stop – 'swim round it' – the next bit may be quite easy. You can always come back and have another try at the obstacle when you've more experience to draw on.

5 Remember that a problem is a problem only until you know what the answer is – then problems disappear.

6 When you feel your morale is low, sit down with a blank sheet of paper, and fill it with things that you already know about what you're learning. You'll be surprised how easy this is.

7 If you find it difficult to go to your study place and resume learning, make yourself a mug of tea or coffee, and go there to enjoy it. Create the association of enjoying a drink with the place where you learn.

8 Don't allow negative feedback from other people to damage your morale. Treat all comments as well-intentioned and useful – and decide which comments are worth taking on board by adjusting your approach.

9 Don't expect your morale to be high every single day. It's perfectly natural to have high days and low days in every part of life, including learning.

10 When you find someone who has the knack of boosting your morale, make increased use of this person – arrange frequent meetings.

them, and to see them several times until we've extracted everything from them that we want or need.

So when, where and with what should we learn?

You've guessed it! – anytime and all the time, anywhere and everywhere, with anything that helps us. The main thing is to *become a learner*. It does not matter when we learn, where we learn, whom we learn from or with or what we learn from or with.

What matters is that we continue to learn, in our own way, at our own pace, at our own places (work, home, and anywhere else that's suitable), and at times of our own choosing. We can learn between shifts, while the kids are at school, while waiting for the washing machine to finish, while waiting for the dinner to cook – there's no 'wrong time' to learn.

Once we become enthused about what we're learning (in other words, have a strong 'want' to learn), everything seems to take care of itself. We learn wherever we are, whenever we can, with whatever helps us, and with whoever helps us. We don't need to go to special places to do our learning then. That said, however important the 'when?', 'where?' and 'with what?' questions are, the fundamental question remains 'how?'. In this chapter, we've pinned down the 'how?' to four key processes – here's a final reminder.

- *wanting to learn:* seeing what the point of it all is
  (or needing to learn)
- *learning by doing:* practising, having a go, including making mistakes
- *positive feelings:* usually based on other people's reactions to what we do
- *'making sense':* 'digesting' what we learn, to gain understanding.

Remember that if sometimes you're a bit stuck in the 'wanting' department, a good strong need will probably do the trick for you. If you can regard a need as a want in disguise – you're winning. Who learns wins!

2

Talent?
What *me*?

We all know people who are talented. Talent comes in many different forms, including intellectual talent, physical talent, linguistic talent, social talent, inventive talent and literary talent. You could probably write a long list of people you know, with various special talents alongside their names. So could they – and *you* would be on *their* lists! We often recognize other people's talents, yet are quite unaware of some of our own best ones. This chapter aims to help put this right!

Will you *never* learn?

How often were you told this? Maybe you're still told this now. I am sometimes! We're usually told this when people are fed up that we've forgotten something, or frustrated that we can't do something. It can (if we're not careful) make us feel that we just have no talent. We may even feel that absolutely everyone else on this planet is cleverer than ourselves, more skilled than ourselves, and more competent than we are. Of course this isn't true, but it sometimes feels like it. In this chapter, we'll explore how we can take stock of our talents.

That little question 'will you never learn?' is probably responsible for a lot of the trouble we have in our minds when we think about learning something. The question implies we're bad at it – or at least that we might not succeed next time we try. The person who asks us this question in an accusatory tone is probably trying (and succeeding often) to give us a very straightforward message:

> 'You're thick! I can do this, I can remember this, I'm better than you. I want to stay better than you, so I'll undermine your confidence, and make sure you never learn it. I want to continue to be one-up on you.'

Think of it like this. 'Will you never learn?' is a deliberate put-down statement. Why should you take notice of it? It's just a small-minded person trying to be a little bigger at your expense. You yourself will be bigger if you don't fall into the trap.

How much have you already learned?

It's funny, but most people don't feel they're particularly good at learning. In fact, when we're learning something new, many of us think we must be *really bad* at learning. And yet, whatever we're learning that's new is only the latest fraction-of-a-percent in what we've already learned in our lives.

Think of everything you now do without having to think. These may include:

- finding your way to various shops for the various items you buy each week
- knowing where (approximately) to look on the supermarket shelves for fresh cauliflowers, aspirin, frozen chips, and sausages (or whatever *your* diet consists of – that was mine)
- knowing where to park the car if you take it into town (or, even more accomplished, being able to get to town on buses, trains or tubes)
- the hundreds of steps that may be involved in preparing or cooking a meal
- working within your budget, and paying for heat, light, food, clothes, and generally 'balancing the books' (or at least knowing how it should be attempted)
- choosing clothes that fit, and washing them and sometimes even repairing them
- keeping your place clean enough and tidy enough to suit you
- attending to the needs of dependants, such as spouses, other relatives, pets, and even kids!
- giving up smoking (this is a major learning achievement, and should have medals or degrees associated with it!)

The list, of course, is endless. Yet all these are vast subjects in themselves. For many of them, there are whole collections of books about how to go about them (including cooking, home-maintenance, budgeting, fashions and clothing, and so on). Yet most of these we can do, without ever having been dependent on any book or learning programme.

The point is that you've already learned an enormous amount of information. You've already acquired a tremendous range of skills and abilities. True, there are things that we all know we can't yet do, but just think for now of everything you *can* do, and *have* done, every day. The amount is vast.

Four kinds of 'competence'

Competence is a rather pleasant word. We're not usually offended if someone describes us as competent. Many learning courses and programmes are now described in competence terms – in other words, information about what people will be able to do when they've successfully completed the programmes. It's useful to take stock of all the competencies you already have, and to put in perspective those that you don't yet have. There are four sides to what we can do, and can't yet do.

(1) Things you know you can already do

All the things that you know you can do could be called your 'conscious competencies'. As we've said, this covers a very wide range indeed, spanning every dimension of your life. We can add more detail about that which we know we can do by using some descriptive words to show how often we do them. We can also add words to describe how well we do them.

Take stock of some of your own competencies now, and fill in some actions to complete the sentences below. Don't forget that these competencies can be in absolutely any part of your life. There's no boundary between academic competencies, sporting competencies, mechanical competencies, personal competencies and social competencies. Everything you can do counts.

1 . . . . :
   I can do this really well.

2 . . . . :
   I do this every day.

3 . . . . :

I can do this when I really have to.

4 . . . . :

I can do well enough for my purposes.

5 . . . . :

I can just about manage to do this.

6 . . . . :

I can do this standing on my head.

You may well have surprised yourself at how easy it was to find six skills you have already mastered. Some of them may be something you find quite easy to do well, but that seem very impressive to other people who can't yet do them.

(2) Things you can already do, but don't realize it yet ('magic'!)

There are also all sorts of activities that you can do, and have done, every day, that you've never actually given any thought to (maybe till now). These could be called your 'unconscious competencies' – something that you're not aware you do, but that you do anyway.

For example, a busy mother with young children will be tackling a wide range of jobs simultaneously; she is highly skilled at 'multitasking'. A coach to a sports team will have keen powers of observation while watching players' performance, and will be able to give detailed comments and advice to each player, but probably will not be aware of how complex either of these tasks is.

See if you can identify three activities you're good at, but that you have not consciously thought about till now. Better still, if you've got a friend or relative you'd like to bring in as your witness, ask them, 'Tell me what I'm actually good at, but don't seem to know it.' You may get some pleasant surprises.

1 . . . .

2 . . . .

3 . . . .

(3) Things you know you can't yet do – targets and goals

What about the other side of the picture? What's the opposite to 'competence'? The most common answer is 'incompetence' – what a nasty word! Have you ever been called 'incompetent'? How did that make you *feel?* All through this book, we're reminding ourselves that learning is a feeling process, and if we're made to feel lousy about it, it's not going to help.

Let's invent a different word for the opposite of competent – 'uncompetent'. This isn't nearly so bad as incompetent. 'Uncompetent' need only mean 'I can't yet do this'. This is perfectly acceptable. The magic word is 'yet' – this word allows hope for what is yet to come. Whenever we learn, we approach something that we can't yet do, then become able to do it.

We all know what we can't yet do. These are our 'conscious uncompetencies' and we are aware of them as possibilities for our future learning. Of course, there are all sorts of things we can't yet do that don't matter at all. For example, I can't run a mile in five minutes. I can't run a mile in a lot more minutes than five but this does not matter – I don't *need* to run a mile. I'm quite happy to walk a mile or even ten miles, and I don't like running, so am not worried that I can't do it.

Try to think of three things that you can't yet do, but that you do want to become able to do. These could be targets for your own learning or personal development.

1 . . . .

2 . . . .

3 . . . .

(4) Things you don't yet know that you can't yet do (danger!)

You might have to read that sub-heading a couple of times. This is another kind of 'uncompetence' that we all share. There are two 'yets' in that sentence. Finding out what we can't yet do is a very important part of learning anything new. Let's call the 'things that we don't yet know we can't yet do' our 'unconscious uncompetencies'. We've all got them – can you think of people around you who don't yet know that they can't yet do something? (I've got a sister-in-law who makes sausage rolls which she thinks are good ones, but everyone else in the family disagrees. She doesn't yet know that she can't yet make good sausage rolls – an 'unconscious uncompetence' – but no-one will tell her, mainly because her apple pies and cheese scones are absolutely excellent.)

The problem with 'things we don't yet know that we can't yet do' is we can be in danger because of them. Sometimes, we only find out about them when there's a crisis or a problem, and we find out too late that we could not act as we would like to have done. However, the positive side of this is that there is no reason why we can't go looking for things we don't yet know we can't yet do. As you may guess, other people are very useful here – they often *do* know what we can't yet do.

See if you can find out three of these things – with help from other people if you can.

1 ....

2 ....

3 ....

Now, if you've written something above, you've actually identified things you can't yet do – but you now know about them. They're not nearly as dangerous when we know what they are.

Notice how important that tiny word 'do' was in all four of those kinds of competence we looked at. Being competent is about being able to do things. In the final analysis, this is more important than just knowing something. Even when we know a lot, no-one can see that we know it unless we show that we know it – and one way or another this involves (you've guessed) *doing* something.

10

TIPS AND WRINKLES | on rewarding yourself

1 Make a list of the top ten things you really enjoy in your everyday life (include foods, drinks, television programmes, or anything else at all!).

2 Check which of these favourite things you will be having or doing today anyway.

3 Resolve that today you're going to earn each of your favourite things by doing a minimum of five minutes and a maximum of ten minutes studying, or practising, or fact-finding before you have them.

4 Notice that you enjoy your favourite things a little bit more when you've done that little bit extra to earn them.

5 Let other people around you in on your tactics. It helps if, for example, when seeing you stop for that cup of tea, someone asks 'now have you done your five minutes worth for this one?'

6 If you've got a video recorder, you can record your favourite programme rather than watch it 'live', and do some learning or practising while the broadcast is on, then watch your video when you reckon you deserve your reward.

7 When you've got into the habit of learning to learn, start matching your rewards to the effort involved in the tasks. Choose substantial tasks for your really favourite rewards.

8 Notice the satisfaction that comes when you weave short spells of learning into the fabric of your everyday life.

9 Keep the long-term rewards in mind as well – think of what it will be like when you've mastered whatever you're wanting to learn.

10 Don't overdo the rewards, however – a 500-gram box of chocolates every time you do an extra few minutes learning may lead you to some problems!

" I think I may need to cut my
learning curve..."

Strengths, weaknesses, opportunities and threats

Next, I'd like you to look at things you can do and things you can't yet do in another way, this time bringing in the important dimension of how you feel about them. The next exercise is based on something that's been around for a long time – 'SWOT Analysis'. ('SWOT' is just the first letters of strengths, weaknesses, opportunities and threats – it's not the swotting you may remember doing for exams.) Let's explore a little about each of the four categories, before you have a go at identifying yours.

Strengths

These are skills we know we have. You looked at one of these in Question 1 in the previous chapter. Strengths are things we know we can do. They can be regarded as our conscious competencies. In addition, our strengths are associated with positive feelings. We feel proud of them. We feel confident about them. We feel pleased about them. Strengths are also evidence of successful learning in the past. They remind us just how much we can learn and have learned.

Weaknesses

These are activities we think we're not good at – or at least not yet. These are our 'conscious uncompetencies'. These include things we can't yet do.

We've often got somewhat negative feelings about our weaknesses. They're things we may feel ashamed of and which may cause us anxiety or apprehension. Yet a weakness is only a weakness until we find out how to master it. We've mastered countless 'weaknesses' all through our lives – and we'll master many more in years to come. So weaknesses are a perfectly natural part of learning. If we did not have any weaknesses, there would be nothing for us to learn.

Opportunities

This is where we can see benefits in store for us; where we have chances to improve our lives. Opportunities are associated with positive feelings and we may feel hope, expectation, even yearning.

In thinking about learning new skills or knowledge, there are always opportunities associated with this. We may be able to move to a more satisfying job, or the increased knowledge may bring greater satisfaction to our everyday lives.

Threats

Again, these are associated with negative feelings, such as feeling vulnerable, or exposed, or open to ridicule. We may fear failure in our learning. Threats are often associated with our self-esteem. If we feel that people may look down on what we're trying to do, we feel so 'threatened' that we may no longer want to try. The threats themselves are often quite hard to pin down – but it is very useful indeed to try to analyze them. In fact, many 'threats' turn out not to be sinister at all, but simply stages to be overcome gently as we move on in our learning and our lives.

When can I use a 'SWOT analysis?'

You can do a 'SWOT analysis' about anything or everything. You can do this sort of analysis to help you decide the pros and cons of moving house. You can use the same technique to help you decide whether to get married (though it does seem a bit unromantic!). You can use this analysis as a way of making sense of your thinking about any important aspect of your life – or indeed any trivial aspect too.

In the exercise which follows shortly, I intended you to apply the 'strengths, weaknesses, opportunities, threats' technique to whatever it is you're currently learning or planning to learn, but use the technique for anything else as well.

Before you start your own analysis, let me give you a couple of examples showing how the analysis can work:

(a) Cheryl and Spanish

Suppose Cheryl is planning to learn Spanish. Her 'SWOT analysis' could contain some of the following components.

Strengths: she enjoys talking to people, and feels good about communicating with them. This will help her to want to become good at speaking Spanish.

Weaknesses: she does not think she's got a good memory, or is good when it comes to grammar. However, she can rationalize these 'weaknesses' by reminding herself that it's not a 'grammar examination' she's going in for, but a real-life situation of communicating with people in Spanish. She can have a dictionary at any time – and people are normally very helpful when they see someone trying to use their language.

Opportunities: the obvious one is that she'll be able to talk to anyone and everyone when she becomes more fluent in spoken Spanish. She'll get much more out of her holidays in Spain. And she'll also find out more about learning languages in general, and who knows, she may sooner or later have another go at French (which she hated at school because of the way it was taught then).

Threats: her bad experience of French at school is still like a cloud in her mind. Also, she's got a job and a family, so not too much spare time to use learning Spanish. However, simply working out what causes these worries is useful in itself – she can now decide that this is going to be quite different to her bad experience with French, and start planning how to put to best use the limited amount of time she has to give to learning Spanish. She can adjust her expectations so that she does not intend to become perfect at Spanish this summer – but will be better next summer and so on.

(b) Ahmed and Art

Ahmed wants to become better able to draw and paint. His family is growing up now, and he has some spare time to devote to learning something new.

Strengths: he has always played about with drawing and painting just for his own amusement. He likes getting people's reactions to sketches he does. People seem to find his work interesting, even though he's never been 'taught' to paint or draw as such.

Weaknesses: he knows he's a bit of a perfectionist, and is never really satisfied with his own efforts. If he tries to sketch something, and it doesn't come out well, he tends not to try any more at that particular topic.

Opportunities: he would like a little sideline to make life more interesting. His job is not always fascinating, and often routine, so he feels he needs a little more stimulus. Learning to paint and draw 'properly' could open new doors for him. He may be able to sell some of his work.

Threats: his wife and sons have never taken his attempts at art seriously. They think he's just playing, even when he knows he's trying really hard. He is concerned that they will not support the idea of him spending some extra time studying how to improve and develop his painting and drawing.

Can you see how identifying strengths, weaknesses, opportunities and threats is a useful first step for Cheryl and Ahmed? They can take positive steps to cope with their weaknesses and threats, and they can use their strengths and the new opportunities to fuel their desire to learn.

Some more uses of 'SWOT Analysis'

The same technique lends itself to a wide variety of uses, including:

- *Problem solving*: start with a problem or challenge. Work out in turn the strengths you can bring to bear on the problem, any weaknesses that may need to be taken care of as you solve the problem, the opportunities that solving the problem will bring you, and also any threats that could get in the way of your solving the problem.

Team analysis: we've so far looked at 'SWOT Analysis' as something you can do by yourself, but a pair, group or team can do it together. Then, everyone contributes their individual strengths, and what matters most is the *combined* strengths when they're all added up. Similarly, each person thinks of their weaknesses, but the weaknesses themselves are less important, as other members of the team may be strong in the areas concerned. The opportunities come in two shapes now; those for the team as a whole, and those for the individuals. The same applies to the threats – the most significant ones are those that affect the team rather than its members.

Your own SWOT analysis

Now it's your turn at last. First of all, think of a proposed action (for example, something you yourself are thinking about learning). Jot down a few words describing your proposed action or development in the box below.

Now, thinking of that action, try to find a few of each of:

- strengths you already have which will help with your action
- weaknesses which you may need to bear in mind as your plan unfolds
- opportunities: 'what's in it for you, when you succeed?'
- threats: factors that could get in the way of your plan

Jot all of these down in the boxes in the grid which follows:

Strengths   **Weaknesses**

Threats   **Opportunities**

Turning Your Analysis into an action plan

Now that you've explored how your learning links to your strengths, weaknesses, opportunities and threats, you can develop your own action plan to maximize your success.

Strengths: find as many ways as you can to use your strengths as you learn. When you're doing something you're good at, you feel positive. The more you make use of your strengths as you learn, the better you will feel about what you're learning, and the more successful you will become at learning.

Weaknesses: take the view that anything you've identified here is not really a weakness – it's just a strength you have not yet developed. Sometimes you can avoid things you're not yet good at altogether. At other times, you may need to tackle that which you can't yet do – but step by step, and one at a time, rather than like a bull at a gate or all at once.

Opportunities: keep reminding yourself of the benefits. Visualize yourself as you will be when you've succeeded at what you're doing. Sense the satisfaction and pride. When you come to a particularly difficult bit in your learning, remind yourself of 'what's in it for you' when you've succeeded. Keep the payoffs in mind.

Threats: keep an eye on these. Often, they're only dangerous to your intended learning if they creep up on you. If you're looking out for them, you can often take evasive action, and stop them interfering with your progress. You may even manage to look at threats in a really positive way – as opportunities in disguise – challenges that are useful learning experiences in their own right.

Getting on with people!

This is one of the most important talents anyone could desire! We all know people we can get on well with – and most of us know at least one person that we just can't seem to see eye-to-eye with. That is the nature of humanity. However, regard any problems with people as a challenge rather than a threat. We can't change them, but we can change ourselves. We can change the way we regard people we don't like too much. We can make the decision that we're going to become able to work with them, and treat them as fellow human beings (even when our instincts may lie towards wishing to subject them to torture and humiliation. We're allowed little trips in our imaginations sometimes!).

'Social skills' are a major asset in any list of our accomplishments or strengths. On a crowded planet, few of us are in a position to work alone, or even to learn alone. Let's remind ourselves of some of the ways that we can fit in with our fellow human beings – even when we don't agree with them, or have the same beliefs.

Be a time lord!

'If only I had time.'
'If only I had more time.'
'If only I had twenty-five hours in a day.'

How often have we said something like this – and heard it said? The

10

TIPS AND WRINKLES | on good social skills

1 Remember that good social skills are not dependent on having done a great deal of learning – some of the most educated people are hopeless socially!

2 Being prepared to like other people is one of the foundations for developing your social skills. Give people the chance to be liked.

3 Everyone likes a good listener – being willing and able to listen is an important social skill.

4 Being able to speak in public is a useful social skill sometimes, but remember that it comes naturally to only a few people – the rest of us have learn it by practising again and again.

5 When working with people, it's as important to be able to be led as to be the leader from time to time.

6 One of the best ways to bolster your own image is to resist all temptation to put anyone else down. (If they need 'putting down', other people around will see it without you resorting to doing it.)

7 The art of being punctual is learned by setting out on the train before the one that should get you there on time!

8 You don't have to like people to be able to work well for them or with them. Focus your attention on the job that is to be done, not on the people who require the job to be done.

9 Remember that all well people have feelings, which are easily hurt (and unwell people are even more easily hurt).

10 Never make assumptions about what other people may be thinking – they may not be thinking at all.

fact is that time is given to each of us in equal measure and no-one has more seconds in a minute than you or I have.

What we need to do is to conquer time. We need to put ourselves in charge of our time rather than letting time control us. It has a lot to do with our attitude towards time, and we can indeed change this.

There are many books and learning packages on 'time management'. Most of these include various exercises to help us discover what we're spending our time on. In fact, we already have a very good idea how our time goes, and there's not usually much to be gained in working out how much time we waste.

It's part of being human to waste time. Don't fight it, accept it. The converse of this is for us to become ever more efficient at using time when we've something definite to achieve. Look at it this way, the better we become at being able to use parts of our time really productively,

" It's alright for you, matey... You haven't spent the whole day multi-tasking..."

10

TIPS AND WRINKLES | on managing your time

1 When you can manage your time well, you can manage anything.

2 We all have the same amount of time to manage – twenty-four hours a day, no more, no less.

3 The art of time management is managing minutes – the hours and the days will then look after themselves.

4 Left to human nature, many things get done in the last 10 per cent of the available time. Therefore, it is quite possible to do them in the *first* 10 per cent of the available time and have a lot of time left over to do even more things.

5 If you've got an important task to do, spend a few minutes doing something non-urgent first. The important task will still get done, but you'll have one less non-urgent task as well.

6 Almost all urgent tasks started life as non-urgent tasks. Stop them becoming urgent by doing them in advance.

7 'If you want a job done well, give it to a busy person': busy people are good enough at time management that they can always do one more job well.

8 It takes less time to clean up your spade after digging your garden than before digging your garden.

9 The better you become at managing your time, the more genuine 'spare time' you will have to enjoy in whatever way you prefer.

10 Pleasures are twice as enjoyable when you've earned the time in which to enjoy them.

the more time we can waste with an easy conscience.

Time is never wasted, really. Even when we've left a job undone for two weeks, we've been gently thinking about it, and putting it into perspective, and when we come back to the job, we are likely to bring to it wisdom and thinking that we would not have been able to bring if we had not 'paused for thought'.

I once wrote for an editor who knew about time. He set his authors deadlines – always on a Tuesday. He knew that they would do a lot of their writing during the final weekend before the deadline (however many weeks they'd had before this) – and put their manuscripts in the post on Monday and he'd get them on Tuesday. He was a 'time lord' – he knew how to manage other people's time! It worked.

The short answer is 'get stuck in, straightaway'. It does not matter what the task is, this strategy works wonders. It allows time for revisions, adjustments, refinements to whatever we do. It also makes us *feel* good! There's nothing like having had a go at a task straightaway – knowing that there is still plenty of time for further work on the task.

3

You've got a sporting chance!

Winners and losers?

This chapter is mainly about physical learning – the sort of learning we do as we improve at activities such as sports, dancing, skating, and a wide range of leisure activities and recreations. Human beings have yet another thing in common with monkeys; we all play. Even learning a musical instrument involves a good deal of development of physical and muscular co-ordination (as well, of course, as the development of the mental processes associated with understanding music, feeling it, and hearing it).

One problem area in this wide field of physical achievements is that there are 'winners and losers'. Individuals win gold medals. Teams win cups and trophies. Winning is great! Everyone likes to win. If we just look at sports and recreations as a 'win or lose' situation, very few of us would bother to participate at all. The chances of winning are not high. The cure for this is to change our own personal definition of 'winning' to 'doing significantly better than I might have done'. That's where learning comes in to it, and (as you will have seen in other parts of this book) we can always improve by learning.

Some negative feelings first!

Sport seems to be an activity which either we love or hate. Some of us (myself included) have very bad memories of sport in general, dating back from my schooldays. My lack of success is easy enough for me to analyze now:

- I wasn't any good at doing sports (I was overweight and unfit!)
- I therefore received very negative comments from other people

whenever I tried to do it and made a mess of it (especially, of course, in team games)
- Because of the bad feedback, and unhappy experiences, when I did try to do it, I just did not want to do it any more, at all, ever!

In short, everything was wrong with how I was learning sports (or athletics, or gymnastics). This was made even worse by the fact that everyone around me seemed good at all of these activities. The fact that I was good at sums was little compensation to me!

Then, the 'lack of want' regarding sport spread further. I became uninterested in watching it – live, or on television – and quite reluctant to even read about it in newspapers or magazines.

Have we to *do* it to learn from it?

'It's no use unless you do it' – how often have we been told this about sports and recreations? There is of course some truth in it. We're not going to exercise our hearts and lungs very much watching people running around on a field – and even less lying on the sofa watching the telly! However, there are many more sides to sport than actually participating. All sorts of people earn their living because of sport, whether they play or participate or just watch. The list includes:

- sports writers, correspondents, editors, commentators
- designers of sports equipment and gear
- manufacturers of everything from socks to helmets
- advertising executives, promoting their products through sports visibility
- trainers, coaches, teachers, physiotherapists
- shop salespeople, market traders, and a few tycoons!
- groundsmen, catering staff, cleaners, ticket staff …

If the only people involved in sports were those participating, probably unemployment would treble! And think of the amount that all these writers, coaches and support staff learn as they go about their jobs.

And the papers are full of it!

I can't think of any newspaper that has not got a sports section. Many newspapers have very extensive sports coverage. It's usually the sports pages that people seem to turn to first – whether to check out a result of a team or competitor, or to see if the football pools have come up. Switch on the television set on a Saturday afternoon, and many channels seem to cover non-stop sports – all analyzed and discussed with an intensity and ardour that seems very profound to someone like me.

Therefore, sport has a lot to do with learning – many people gain a lot of their reading skills because of sport. Let's face it, everything is right for them to develop such skills:

- they're interested, therefore they want to read
- they practise reading about something they're keen to find out about
- they get plenty of feedback as they compare what they've found out with what other people have read about
- even the 'making sense' stage of learning is catered for, as people see on television, or hear on radio, something they've been reading about

Sports addicts hooked on radio and television coverage learn a further range of life skills from their addiction:

- they improve their time management as they strive to be in the right place at the right time for a broadcast
- they improve their 'dealing with machines' skills as they learn to program the video to catch a match for later
- they improve their 'learning from watching others' skills and their listening skills

Everyone seems to talk about it!

One is regarded as mentally deficient if one is unaware of the details of the recent performances of the local team, or National teams, or famous athletes and sportspersons. Far more people know who leads the England team (at whatever sport) than know the name of the current Secretary of State for Education! So sport is often intimately linked to the development of our communication skills. This in turn helps us to develop social skills.

We've already seen that sport is a major source of learning and an aid to developing skills for a wide range of people who may never participate directly themselves, and, of course, for the participants too.

Simply not cricket!

We've been thinking about sport for a while, but there are all sorts of other activities that are similar to sports, athletics or games in some respects.

What do all the following have in common?

- ballet dancing
- playing the piano
- playing in a pop group
- gardening
- wallpapering
- disco dancing

They've got *several* elements in common:

1   They all involve developing physical skills.
2   They all depend to some extent on timing and control (particularly wallpapering!).
3   They all have behind them whole industries of teachers, writers, suppliers, manufacturers, and so on – besides the people who actually engage in the activities themselves.
4   They all have to be learned; we don't start life already programmed to do these things without at least some investment in ourselves.
5   Most people who do them, do so because they enjoy doing them – this links to wanting to learn to do them in the first place.
6   All of these things are learned by practising – and particularly by getting them wrong at first.
7   Other people's reactions are important for everyone doing any of these activities – positive feedback produces positive feelings.
8   They are all learned a bit at a time – we need to make sense of them as we go along – we need time to 'digest' our learning experiences.

Goals and targets

Whether you're interested in sports, games, artistic activities like music or painting and drawing, or any of the skills we've mentioned so far in this chapter, if you're going to get actively involved you need goals and targets. In fact, all of life is really about goals and targets. These words may have come from sports like football or archery, but they apply to everything. You've heard the expression 'if you don't know where you're going, any bus will do'. Many aspects of life are like this. The better we know where we're going, the more likely we are to get there.

In any physical activity (from dancing to Olympic sports) it's important that goals and targets are not too high. We need to move one step at a time. Targets need to be reasonable. Our goals need to be achievable.

Let's suppose you were aiming to be a high-jump world record holder; you would be unlikely to break the record by going and giving it your best shot here and now. A more sensible approach would be to spend a bit of time today seeing what your present best shot is. Then tomorrow, see if you can manage that same target more than once, and keep on next day and next day till you can. Then raise the height by a centimetre, and see how you get on.

Love hurts!

If you've never been in love, you probably won't believe this. If you have – you'll know it. When we're in love, our emotions are very strong. Physically and mentally we change – our urges and drives and hormones all leapfrog with each other. We often have wild swings between extreme happiness and deep anxiety or tension. Much of this is due to us being particularly aware of our feelings at such times. When we're particularly sensitive due to heightened emotions, it's surprisingly easy for our feelings to be hurt. That's normally the sort of 'hurt' people think about when they see the phrase 'love hurts!'.

However, our bodies can hurt too. 'Pain' is a four-letter word that we all know the meaning of.

What ever happened to the bloke who used to catch the bus to go crocodile wrestling?

We can buy painkillers at the supermarket or pharmacy. Doctors can give us more powerful painkillers if we've got more powerful pains in our bodies. So what is pain? It's hard to describe really. It can be anything from a dull ache to a sharp pang. It can be anything from a stab now and then to continuous extreme discomfort. We could say that pain is nature's way of telling us that there is something wrong. Pain often prevents us from doing something that would cause us further damage. If we accidentally touch something that's very hot, we feel pain and immediately try to get away from the heat. We even learn through this mistake, and try harder to avoid very hot objects for quite some time.

In many sports and recreations, pain seems to be part of the picture. When we've exercised more strenuously than before, we often experience quite a lot of pain and stiffness in our muscles and joints. This pain is quite natural, but is still pain. It still hurts. Rather than reach for the painkillers, however, we often say: 'It hurts, so it must be doing me good'. The pathway to fitness is often quite a painful one, but when we get there it was worth the pain (we claim).

It's all in your mind?

Sometimes when we've got a pain we're told this. Sometimes it's true. In a way we could say that it's always true – it's our brain that experiences pain. It might be my toe that's damaged, but it's my brain that feels the pain. With sports and recreation, however physical the effort

" Keep away! Keep away! If it's hurting this much it must be doing me good..."

and exercise, the mind remains very important indeed.

To maximize our successes, we have to strive with our minds as well as with our muscles. Successful athletes know how important mind over matter is. The will to succeed needs to be in the mind, to be passed to the muscles.

If we think back to our discussion about learning, the four stages we looked at in Chapter 1 are involved in their own way in sports and physical activities.

Wanting

If we really want to achieve our goals or targets, we're much more likely to succeed. You will have seen people around you do something you never thought they could do, and something that they themselves may not have imagined they could do. One factor in cases like this is usually a very strong will to succeed.

Learning by doing, practising, making mistakes

Sports and recreational activities *are* doing things. If we engage in them, we can't help learning by doing. If we're really keen on them we do them a lot, and set ourselves demanding training targets. The importance of learning from our mistakes is as useful as ever. When we're just setting out to do something we've not yet done, we don't expect to get it absolutely right today – or tomorrow. We learn from how it goes today, we'll learn a bit more tomorrow, and so on. Our bodies learn from the experience of trying, and our minds learn at the same time.

Other people's reactions – feedback

This is probably more important when we're developing our sports and physical skills than in any other kind of learning. We'll explore this in more detail a bit later.

Making sense of the experience – and of the feedback

When we're learning physical activities, we need to 'digest' our experiences. We need to get our minds around what our bodies are doing, and about what we're finding out about our performance, from our own bodies, and from anyone else who can help. It all comes back to gathering feedback. But who can give us feedback? By now, I hope you'll feel that anyone and everyone can give us at least some feedback on our performance, and that no feedback is without use.

Let's next look at a special person whose role is to be 'on our side' and to give us personal feedback. A useful term for such people is 'mentors'. Have you one (or more)? I'm lucky, I've got two at the moment. Without them, I'd never have managed to write this book.

Get yourself a mentor

In any physical activity, other people can tell us a great deal about ourselves. Experienced instructors and coaches develop an expert eye for ways we could try to make our performance better. They develop ways of explaining to us what we should try to do. If we get on the defensive, however, and reject their observations, criticisms or suggestions, we are likely to miss out on an important source of help and support.

Sometimes an instructor or a coach can also be a mentor. However, it may be best to find a completely independent mentor. So what exactly is a mentor? What does a mentor do?

In short, a mentor has the following characteristics:

- someone we trust and feel we know
- someone whose views and opinions we respect
- someone who has our best interests and performance at heart
- someone who is willing and able to give us feedback
- someone who is essentially 'on our side'
- someone who will help us plan our actions
- someone who will firmly (but kindly) keep our noses to the grindstone

A mentor does not have to be an expert in what you're learning. Sometimes, it can be very useful to have a mentor who can't do what you're trying to do. In such circumstances, your mentor may be all the more understanding of the problems you encounter, and the difficulties you experience on the journey to success.

Essentially, a mentor is a friend – but a friend with a definite purpose – to help you step-by-step work towards the achievement of your goals. A mentor is someone who will call in to see you unexpectedly and ask, 'how is it going then?'. A mentor is someone who will ring you up and ask, 'how are you getting on?'.

A mentor is someone who is entirely 'in' on your targets and plans. A mentor is someone you can speak to in confidence – and someone you can vent your feelings to when you're frustrated, annoyed, or

10

TIPS AND WRINKLES | on choosing and using a mentor

1 Choose someone you get on with and respect – they don't have to be an expert in the area you're learning.

2 Choose someone you feel comfortable with – someone you can talk to about your feelings as well as about what you're learning.

3 Choose someone you have easy access to – someone whom you can meet regularly and at short notice when necessary.

4 Regard your mentor as a trusted friend rather than a teacher. Your mentor should be 'on your side' as you learn.

5 Arrange definite meetings with your mentor. The sheer fact that you've got such a meeting coming up can be a spur to you and help you make progress with your learning.

6 Agree targets with your mentor. Work out between you what you should try to be able to do between now and the next meeting.

7 Listen to your mentor – don't be defensive. All feedback is useful.

8 When you have problems with your learning, let your mentor help you to work out between you exactly what the problems are, and how you may choose to go about solving them.

9 Show your mentor that you value the support you receive. That way you're likely to get even more.

10 Remember to thank your mentor when you've completed your learning and let your mentor share in your success.

disappointed. A good mentor is someone who chooses to forget quickly something you have said in the heat of the moment.

A mentor is a source of good feedback. You may also have expert feedback from coaches or trainers.

Let's try out an exercise on giving and taking feedback next.

Exercise on giving and receiving feedback

For this exercise, you will need one more person. This can be anyone: a friend; a partner; a colleague; or a complete stranger. It will only take about five minutes. If you've got another person to try it out with do it now – otherwise save it till you have the opportunity. Do the following steps one at a time, without looking ahead please – or you'll spoil the effects for yourself. Both of you do each step.

Step 1
Don't say anything yet, but think *of a compliment about each other.* (This can be anything at all. Not a sound should be made by either of you while you're doing this – just a few seconds silent thought.)

Step 2
Say *your compliments to each other in turn.*

Step 3
Look back on how this went.

You probably found it a bit embarrassing. Many people when they receive a compliment laugh. In this situation, laughter seems to be a sort of defence mechanism, and we use it to protect us from further embarrassment. We often try to shrug off the compliment. We say things such as:

- oh, it's nothing really
- well, it just happens that it's a good day for me
- think nothing of it, it's not special

Now think what is happening. The person *giving* the compliment is effectively being choked off. The compliment is being rejected or belittled. That's hardly going to encourage further compliments. And the person receiving the compliment is not really taking the compliment on board. The compliment is being thrown away. Next try it another way – try Step 4.

Step 4
Say the compliments again to each other, but this time accepting them (for example, saying 'thank you for that' or 'I'm so glad you like that').

It feels a little strange at first. But with practice it gets quite natural to *accept* compliments freely. Feel yourself swell with pride as you take on board compliments rather than shrug them off. Remember how important other people's comments are when it comes to us developing positive feelings.

A further benefit of ready acceptance of compliments is that people giving us such positive feedback are no longer choked off. It's easier for them to give us positive feedback, so we'll get more of it. The British are particularly bad at accepting compliments – many other cultures don't have as much of a problem in this area.

Step 5
Think of (but don't say) *a criticism about each other.*

Step 6
Now say *your criticisms to each other.*

'Ouch', we feel. Criticisms can hurt. They are negative feedback. But remember how much we learn from our mistakes. Criticisms are very useful feedback. The criticisms may sometimes be unjust, and in such cases we should not feel hurt. When the criticisms are fair, we should not be hurt at all, but pleased to be informed of useful feedback which we may not otherwise have been alerted to. One way of thinking of it is, 'there is no such thing as criticism, only feedback'. Is there a way out of this situation? Finally, try Step 7.

Step 7
Say again your criticisms to each other, this time accepting them (for example, using phrases such as, 'Thanks for telling me that', or 'That will be useful for me to bear in mind, thanks'.

As with compliments, we can train ourselves to accept criticism. If we listen patiently to critical comments rather than choke off those giving us them, we get much more feedback. People making critical comments often start rather tentatively, and give a gentle criticism to see whether they really dare tell us about the thing that we really should be told about. If we reject their gentle criticisms, we'll certainly never benefit by finding out the bigger ones.

Go fishing

You've heard the phrase 'fishing for compliments' where people are deliberately hoping to hear positive comments about themselves. There's no real harm in that of course – except that when people know we're looking too earnestly for compliments, they sometimes get tired of giving us them.

It's equally possible to fish for negative feedback. When someone starts to give you some critical comment, don't stop them in their tracks by becoming hostile or offended. Open the doors to further comment. When the criticism stops, look for more by asking gently, 'thanks, now are there any further things you've noticed on that?' or 'good, I'm glad you told me that, now which would you suggest is the first thing I should try to improve there?'

When receiving critical or positive feedback, the key thing is to keep listening, and not to be the one to break the silence when one point has been made. Let people continue to tell you anything and everything they have to tell you. Draw it out of them. Help them to explain themselves to you. 'How exactly do you see me doing this?' 'Is there anything else you can help me with?'

That's the spirit!

Many sporting and recreational activities are team games. Team activities, besides the development of physical skills and abilities, require development of the whole mind too. When being interviewed for jobs, people are often asked about their participation in leisure activities. It's a good thing to be able to claim that you're part of a team (any sort of team), as it shows potential employers that you can get on with people, and like being with people.

Team spirit involves a wide range of feelings and processes, including:

- not wanting to let the side down, and doing the best we can

10

TIPS AND WRINKLES | on listening

1 Many people confess to be 'hard of hearing'. Many, many more are 'hard of listening'.

2 God gave most of us two ears. He did not, however, intend us to use one for things to go in, and the other for things to go out.

3 If you have some questions already in your mind, you will hear the answers when you come to them.

4 It is difficult to speak and listen at the same time – you tend to hear only what you say.

5 When you're listening really well, you're normally doing something with what you hear, such as making notes of it, making decisions about it, or working out questions to ask about it.

6 Everyone likes a good listener.

7 Some people only hear what they want to hear. Good learners hear what they want to find out.

8 Practise active listening even when you don't need to. Try making mental notes of the main points from a news broadcast, and finding out how many of them you can remember after an hour or so.

9 When you hear some information, work out what question the information is the answer to. Remembering the questions helps you remember what you hear.

10 Decide what you don't wish to remember as you listen. Deliberately rejecting the unimportant helps you retain more of what is useful.

10

TIPS AND WRINKLES | on positive feelings and emotions

1 Remind yourself how useful it is to feel positive about things you're learning.

2 Take every chance to gather positive feedback on your performance at skills you're learning.

3 When someone pays you a compliment about how well you're doing, don't shrug it off saying 'Oh, it's nothing really'; instead, accept the compliment and swell with pride, saying 'Thank you for that.'

4 If you find you have negative feelings or emotions, try to pinpoint the exact origin of these feelings, then assert that you're not going to allow yourself to be put off by such feelings.

5 Remember when coping with negative feelings or emotions that all such feelings are transient. You will feel better about whatever it is tomorrow, or next week, or next month. Give your feelings time to settle.

6 Keep reminding yourself of all the things you can already do, rather than dwelling on one or two things you can't yet do.

7 When you come across something that you think you can't do, remind yourself that it's something you can't yet do, not something that you can't ever do.

8 Many of the things we find we can't yet do turn out to be things that we don't need to do anyway – don't allow such things to damage your feelings or emotions.

9 If you're feeling low about something that's gone wrong with your learning (or your life in general), be patient with people who say 'Come on, pull yourself together now.' Sooner or later, they'll find out for themselves that it's easier said than done!

10 Remember that time is the big healer for damaged feelings and emotions. 'No-one will care about that in a hundred years' a wise colleague once advised me when I was feeling cheesed off!

- wanting to help other people in the team
- being able to communicate effectively with fellow team members
- being able to give and take feedback, whether positive or critical
- sharing a common goal with other people
- sometimes working collaboratively, and not competitively, within the team

All of these feelings and processes are every bit as valuable in day-to-day life as in sports and recreations. Getting on with our neighbours, getting on with our workmates or colleagues – and getting on with our relatives (sometimes the hardest one!) all benefit from the feelings and processes that make for good team spirit.

Healthy body, healthy mind?

In a way, the whole of life is a team game. Sometimes we may be competing to try to be the best in the team. At other times, it is enough that we play our part in the team, and provide support to the other members. It often helps us to keep physically fit and well using sports and recreations as our source of exercise, and helping us to get on well with other people in the process. There is nothing quite like getting healthily tired, for making our minds put other areas of our lives into a healthy perspective.

To improve at any sport or recreation is something we can be proud of – it's a positive learning achievement. The learning involves both mind and body. Our brains learn to control our muscles to give us the necessary skills and co-ordination, and our muscles learn to respond to the stimulus of targets and goals, and to deliver the performance we want from them. In a way, sports and recreations are the most complete learning experiences we have – they involve our whole beings – including our feelings and emotions, as well as our skills and abilities. It is exactly this sort of learning that helped us evolve from the monkeys, as successfully competitive beings, able to take ever more control of ourselves and our environment.

4

Just not mechanically-minded?

How do you eat an elephant?

The only way would be one bite at a time! (Not that I've ever eaten an elephant I hasten to add as an instinctive vegetarian!) This chapter is about following instructions and becoming more confident about your abilities to do mechanical activities that you never thought you dare try. I hope that also I can help you take credit for many complex tasks that you already do and have never really thought about.

The nature of instructions is that they usually come as a series of steps, to be carried out one after the other. If we get one step wrong, it's quite likely that things may go wrong thereafter. Many of us have instructions to follow in our jobs. We may follow even more instructions in our day-to-day lives. In this chapter, we'll take a little diversion to look at just how many problems words can give us, if the words are not well-chosen and well-considered. This will lead into more detailed thoughts about how best to use words in the next two chapters.

How do you get on with mechanical things?

Many people think they just don't get on with practical tasks and physical objects. *'Oh no, not me! I just don't get on with mechanical things or electrical things. I don't try to do anything like that. I don't buy self-assembly furniture, and make the pieces come to reality with a screwdriver and hammer in my back yard or living room! The only way is for me to get someone in to do it for me.'*

We've all met people who say something similar to this. However,

when we start analyzing it, almost everyone who claims they are not good at following complex instructions in one area of life is already good at following equally complex ones in another.

Go on, just do as you're told!

This is the essence of following instructions. It goes against human nature somewhat; none of us like being in the position of doing what we're told! We've all been told to do this far too often earlier in our lives. We prefer to do it our way. And we usually do. However, the people who write instructions usually know what they are talking about, and it is wise to give up our personal pride and prejudice, and to

Quiz on 'Getting things done'

How good are you at using your hands, brain (and tools) while following instructions, setting up machines, following recipes in your kitchen, putting together components and so on? For each of the following, decide whether you're 'highly skilled', 'muddle along eventually' or 'wouldn't touch it with a bargepole'. There are no wrong answers!

		I'm good at this	I can muddle along with this	Wouldn't touch it with a bargepole
1	I can put together a self-assembly set of drawers.			
2	I can connect up a new video recorder.			
3	I can make a good 'celebration cake' and often get commissioned to make them for friends.			
4	I can install a new dishwasher to the existing plumbing in my kitchen.			
5	I can climb into someone else's car and work out how to drive it.			
6	I can make most of my own clothes, including fancy evening dresses, if I want to.			
7	I can replace a washer on a dripping tap without flooding the house!			
8	I can manage the household accounts efficiently and smoothly, and keep the books balanced.			
9	I can replace the lock on my front door when my keys are stolen or lost.			
10	I can pick a good holiday package abroad, make all the arrangements and organize us getting there smoothly.			

try to do it *their* way. After all, they're not personally watching us; the instructions are usually in print. And even when they *are* there watching us, if we get it wrong using *their* instructions, whose fault is it? Not ours, of course! So what have we to lose? Before we start looking at how best to follow instructions and get things done, see how you rate at our quiz on the previous page.

Responses to 'Getting things done' quiz

We've all got our strengths and weaknesses when it comes to 'do-it-yourself'. Some of us actually enjoy sorting matters out for ourselves. Others would rather do anything to avoid having to do it ourselves.

What's in common between all of the jobs mentioned in our quiz? Three things:

- they're all practical tasks
- they can all be done one step at a time by following a series of well-written instructions
- many ordinary people excel at one or more of them – yet think nothing of it

1   *I can put together a self-assembly set of drawers.*
    You may be surprised at the unlikely people who can manage to put together self-assembly furniture. All it needs is patience and confidence. Anyone who can follow a knitting pattern, make a dress or follow a complex recipe has all that it takes to follow this sort of set of instructions.

2   *I can connect up a new video recorder.*
    The main thing is not to be frightened of the machine. Also, don't expect that it will all go like clockwork. Sometimes we have to play around for quite some time to find out (for example) how to tune-in a video recorder to our local television channels. However, it is very rare that you would do anything that would actually damage the machine, so feel able to give it a go – learn by doing, and by trial and error.

3   *I can make a good 'celebration cake' and often get commissioned to make them for friends.*

This sort of skill is often underrated by people who have it. It involves: following step-by-step instructions; using your judgement, to make adaptations as you go; all sorts of timing skills; using a range of equipment, and so on. If you can do all of this, there is very little else that you could not do.

4   *I can install a new dishwasher to the existing plumbing in my kitchen.*
This one is rather harder – mainly because it's the sort of thing we would only do very occasionally. However, if there's no new plumbing to be done, you don't need to be a plumber to do it. It may simply be a case of making a few connections to existing piping with plastic hoses . And if all the water is turned off, nothing disastrous can go wrong.

5   *I can climb into someone else's car, and work out how to drive it.*
Many people who don't claim to be mechanically-minded can (and do) quickly turn their hands to driving vehicles quite different from the ones they are used to. In fact, doing just this demonstrates a very wide range of physical and mechanical skills.

6   *I can make most of my own clothes, including fancy evening dresses if I want to.*
If you can do this, don't let anyone tell you you're not mechanically-minded. The care and precision which goes into cutting fabric to exact patterns is a major factor in any engineering feat.

7   *I can replace a washer on a dripping tap without flooding the house!*
This may not seem a difficult task to anyone who has done it several times before, but it can appear quite impossible to anyone who has never done it. It's like most other things – once we've done it ourselves, it's not a problem any more. With some precautions (such as turning the water supply off properly) there's very little to go wrong.

8   *I can manage the household accounts efficiently and smoothly, and keep the books balanced.*
Millions of people do just this, and do it well. Yet do they give

themselves credit for the skills involved. These skills include handling numbers, but also include much more sophisticated skills such as strategic planning, forecasting, decision-making and record-keeping.

9   *I can replace the lock on my front door when my keys are stolen or lost.*
    With a bit of planning, you don't have to be highly skilled at woodwork to do a job like this. It's not usually too difficult to get the old lock off, and if you take the old lock to the hardware shop, you're usually able to get one of the same size, so that you can use the existing holes in your woodwork to fit the new one.

10 *I can pick a good holiday package abroad, make all the arrangements and organize us getting there smoothly.*
    Several million people manage this every year. But do they give themselves credit for just how complex a task they have succeeded at? They will have made all manner of choices and decisions in the process, organized currency, organized getting to the port or airport on time, as well as the myriad of decisions about what to take, what to wear, and what to do when they get there.

Additional Comments

All of those jobs *could* be done my most of us, if we really had to do them, and if we had a really good set of instructions, or a clear set of guidelines. Indeed, many of us already do several of those jobs without thinking anything special about it. Yet all of those tasks are the bread-and-butter work of people who do them every day – plumbers, electricians, accountants, chefs, dressmakers, travel agents, and so on. They become specialists in the various tasks, and don't any longer need to read any instructions or follow the recipes. That's evidence of another kind of learning. These specialists are all well-versed in their trades or skills, and have learned them by practising at them – and by making mistakes at first. They've probably learned many parts of their jobs by following instructions at the start, and by watching other people showing them how to do the tasks.

However, for most of us, every now and then we need to be able to have a go at jobs of this sort that we have not tackled ever before, armed with a set of instructions or a recipe book or a guide. That's what this chapter is about: ways of making sense of sets of printed instructions and advice; developing our confidence to handle equipment or information; and keeping our cool as we learn the natural way – by trial and error.

Safety first!

Before you embark with renewed confidence to tackle something you've never tried before, especially mechanical or electrical jobs, think of your personal safety, and that of anyone else who may be affected if something were to go wrong. This is not a book about safety, however, to win at your learning, you've got to make sure you survive. So I apologize for straying for a page or two from the business of learning to look at practical tasks, but I hope that you will find some of the comments which follow not only useful, but in your personal interest.

Electricity

If you're going to do anything with electrical circuits (for example, replace a single wall socket with a double one), a few simple points will guarantee your safety:

- Turn the power off at the main fuse box, so that the part of the circuit you are working on is not 'live'.
- Having turned off the power, check that the power really is off! Switch the light on to check it doesn't light up, or plug something into the socket to check it is indeed isolated.
- Even when you know it should be safe, there's no shame in wearing rubber gloves anyway. And don't wear wet ones – electricity and water are a dangerous combination.
- Use a 'mains detector' screwdriver, and check now and then that the power is still off!
- When you've finished the job, plug something in to the new part of the circuit while the power is still switched off, and only then go to the fuse box and restore the supply. It's far better to be miles away at the moment of truth – just in case for one reason or another there is a little explosion in your new circuit! And of course if you hear a bang or see a flash, if you're at the fuse box you're in the best place possible to switch everything off safely.

Water

Water is not as dangerous as electricity – few people drown because of their attempts at a bit of plumbing going wrong. However, water moves quickly and seems to get everywhere if something goes wrong, and the most dangerous place that water can get is into your electric circuits – then water *can* kill. A few steps to take before doing anything with the water system (or central heating radiators) are as follows:

- Make sure you know where the water mains stopcock is, and check that turning it off actually turns the supply right off! Quite often, stopcocks don't stop the flow completely. If this is the case, you may find that turning on the 'lowest' cold water tap in your house or flat will allow any small flow of water to escape harmlessly, and prevent water flowing beyond that point.
- If you're doing a job where there is that possibility that something may go wrong and you may end up having to get someone to do it for you, don't start after dinner on a Friday night, or on a Bank Holiday Monday – help is not readily available at such times! A weekday morning is the best time to start something that may just go wrong.
- If you're changing a washer on a cold water tap, check that there is not any water flowing when you turn the tap on. Sometimes, the supply may come from a storage tank and not from the mains, in which case you may have to find yet another stopcock somewhere in the system before you can start taking the tap to bits.
- If you're doing anything with a hot water tap, you'll probably need to find a stopcock somewhere between the hot water tank and the tap. You probably won't need to turn the cold water mains off in such cases (though there's no harm in being certain).
- If you're doing anything at all with hot water systems (including radiators), make sure that any fire or heating boiler which heats the water has been off for some time before you start, and stays off while you work. (Heating up an empty boiler can turn out to be really expensive!).
- A simple tip – but a useful one: if you're changing a tap washer, put the plug into the bath or sink you're working at. This stops any little screws you happen to take out of the tap disappearing down the plughole forever!
- If, say, corroded taps are 'too stiff', don't go any further. Don't try to force anything while unscrewing components. If you apply too much force, you may rupture the piping system to which the tap is connected, and then you will definitely need to call in a professional to sort it out for you (and won't be able to use the system till you can get help).
- If you've not changed a tap washer before, there are two courses of action. Probably the best is to get someone to talk you through it, asking them to make *you* do it, rather than show you how *they* do

it. The second-best choice is to look up how to do it in a do-it-your-self manual. This is only second-best because of the variety of different kinds of taps – somehow the ones pictured in the manuals never are quite the same as your taps.

Gas

My advice here is quite simple – don't do it! If you have the slightest suspicion that anything is wrong with your gas system, call in the experts. They can detect tiny traces of gas in the air, and if you think you've a leak the best thing is to turn off the supply at your meter, then call them out. The problem with gas is that if there is something wrong, the gas itself can travel long distances between walls, above ceilings, under floors, and sooner or later there is the possibility of a very large bang which may affect the whole building. Besides the risk to yourself, you could face a very large insurance claim if your attempt to install a new gas boiler blew up the flat upstairs as well as yours!

But instructions are only words!

Next, let's move on to something that can be more dangerous than gas, electricity or water – *words!* Even the most complicated set of instructions is made up of a series of sentences composed of words.

Sometimes the words are spoken. Then we have the benefit of hearing: the tone of voice; the emphasis; the facial expression of the speaker; and the body language – all of which can add a lot to our understanding of what the instructions actually mean in practice. At other times, the words are in print. Then, we do not have the benefits which go with spoken instructions. We're on our own. We've got to make sense of the words. We've got to follow the instructions one step at a time – usually on our own – until we find we're succeeding (or failing) to get the task 'right'. This is harder – if more common.

There are all sorts of books and manuals which exhort us to 'do it ourselves'. What this means in practice is to do something without feedback from other people as we're trying to do whatever it is. We have to rely on our senses of sight and sound to gain feedback on whether we're following the instructions successfully. When the drawers don't fit into the slots, we know that we've messed up on an instruction somewhere along the line.

Have a go at the exercise on the next page. I should say that the

Exercise on 'What really happened?'

Given the story below, you have ten minutes to record in the space provided beside each statement whether it is 'true', 'false' or you 'don't know'. (Mark with an x.) Add up your scores in each column when you have finished.

A business man had just turned off the lights in a store when a man appeared and demanded money. The owner opened up a cash register. The contents of the cash register were scooped up and the man sped away. A member of the police force was notified promptly.

	True	False	Don't know
1 A man appeared after the owner had turned off his store lights.			
2 The robber was a man.			
3 The man who appeared did not demand money.			
4 The man who opened the cash register was the owner.			
5 The store owner scooped up the contents of the cash register and ran away.			
6 Someone opened a cash register.			
7 After the man who demanded money scooped up the contents of the cash register, he ran away.			
8 While the cash register contained money, the story does not state how much.			
9 The robber demanded money of the owner.			
10 The robber opened the cash register.			
11 After the store lights were turned off a man appeared.			
12 The robber did not take the money with him.			
13 The robber did not demand money of the owner.			
14 The owner opened a cash register.			
15 The age of the store owner was not revealed in the story.			
16 Taking the contents of the cash register with him, the man ran out of the store.			
17 The story concerns a series of events in which only three persons are referred to: the owner of the store; a man who demanded money; and a member of the police force.			
18 The following events were included in the story: someone demanded money, a cash register was opened, its contents were scooped up, and a man dashed out of the store.			

exercise has some history. Parts of it were developed in the United States in the 1970s by Pfeiffer and Jones. Since then, many people including me have had their hands on the words – and added more words – and on the interpretations of the words, until this present version of mine.

Can I say at the outset, however, that it's not 'getting the right answer' that matters most, but what we can learn about ourselves through getting the wrong answers. Well, you've had all the clues I'm going to give you just yet, and the moment of truth has arrived – you're on your own now. Follow the instructions that I have provided for the task as set out on the page opposite.

How did you do? Did you decide 'true' 'false' and 'don't know' for each of the 18 statements about the story in the box?

Well, there were several possibilities wrapped up in the words of the story in the box. In fact, the words are full of ambiguities. We don't know whether the business man was the owner. Indeed, we don't know whether the owner might have been a woman and not a man. Above all, we don't know that there was a robbery. The following scenario shows a different set of possibilities – all within the information you have been given so far.

I've run this exercise with thousands of people face-to-face – people from all walks of life and of all ages. Very few people come to the 'right answer' straightaway, all by themselves. The only people to do this tend to be people whose job requires that they are very skilled at interpreting words in print – for example editors. Members of Her Majesty's Constabulary distinguish themselves by having scores such as 9, 9, 0 or 13, 5, 0 or 6, 12, 0! I'll leave you to work out why this is – I have my own theory – but it is not wise for me to share it in print here!

Before you read on to find out what the 'correct' answers are, you may like to reflect on what you've done with the exercise. Better still, you may like to work through the exercise with someone else. Remember how important it is to get other people's comments and reactions on decisions that we make.

What I would really like you to do, is to come to a firm decision about the scores you give to the 'true', 'false' and 'don't know' options, before you read on to find out which scores are 'correct'.

In fact, there is not an absolutely correct answer. However, within

What actually happened!

A security firm collected the takings from the store owner to take to the bank. The owner, a businessman, was just closing up and switching off the lights at the time. He rang the police station as a routine procedure.

		True	False	Don't know
1	A man appeared after the owner had turned off his store lights.			X
2	The robber was a man.			X
3	The man who appeared did not demand money.		X	
4	The man who opened the cash register was the owner.			X
5	The store owner scooped up the contents of the cash register and ran away.			X
6	Someone opened a cash register.	X		
7	After the man who demanded money scooped up the contents of the cash register, he ran away.			X
8	While the cash register contained money, the story does not state how much.			X
9	The robber demanded money of the owner.			X
10	The robber opened the cash register.			X
11	After the store lights were turned off a man appeared.	X		
12	The robber did not take the money with him.			X
13	The robber did not demand money of the owner.			X
14	The owner opened a cash register.	X		
15	The age of the store owner was not revealed in the story.	X		
16	Taking the contents of the cash register with him, the man ran out of the store.			X
17	The story concerns a series of events in which only three persons are referred to: the owner of the store; a man who demanded money; and a member of the police force.			X
18	The following events were included in the story: someone demanded money, a cash register was opened, its contents were scooped up, and a man dashed out of the store.			X
	Totals	**4**	**1**	**13**

the limitations of the precision of mere words, it is possible to make out a case for the best possible choices of options. When you're quite sure you don't want to make any further adjustments to your own score, look at the facing page.

So what can we learn from this?

As you will have seen from the different version of the 'story' in the box, there was more than one possibility for what had actually happened. There may indeed have been a robbery, however, we were not given enough information to know that this was the case. In fact, this exercise is more about what we don't know than what we do know. There are several points which this devious little exercise shows. Here are some of them – no doubt on the basis of your own attempt at the exercise you'll be able to add to the list that follows:

1 *It's dangerous to make assumptions!*
   Every time you chose a 'true' or a 'false' option when it turned out to be a 'don't know' option, the reason was that you were led into making some kind of assumption. The same applies to following any kind of instruction. Only if you really know exactly what the instruction means, are you able to follow the instruction properly. It's human nature to make assumptions. However, it's always dangerous. One colleague once pointed out that the word 'assume' could be thought of as 'ass – you – me'. In other words, making an assumption could make both you and me seem like asses!

2 *It's useful to talk to other people*
   If you did that exercise with one or more other people, you would no doubt get into discussion. 'Was there really a robbery?' someone may have asked. 'Was the businessman the same person as the owner?' someone could have asked. Each time, you would have identified one more thing that you did not know from the information given – you would have tracked down a problem. A group of people is more likely to 'crack' this exercise than an individual working alone.

3 *We prefer to know, rather than be found 'not knowing'!*
   Almost everyone I have run this exercise with has underestimated what they 'don't know'. It's more comfortable to say 'true' or 'false'

than 'don't know'. We instinctively feel there's something wrong with us if we have to admit 'don't know'. Yet in this exercise, in thirteen instances, 'don't know' was the best possible choice. What this means is that it is very useful – and very important – for us to confront what we 'don't know'. In fact, when people approach this exercise with the view, 'what *don't* I know about each statement?', they almost always make no mistakes at all. It's always useful to be on the lookout for what we don't yet know.

4   *The wording of task instructions is crucial!*
In that exercise, the wording to the task instructions was as unhelpful as I could make it. Remind yourself of the actual words in the instructions:

Given the story below, you have ten minutes to record in the space provided beside each statement whether it is 'true', 'false' or you 'don't know'. (Mark with an x.) Add up your scores in each column when you have finished.

Not helpful! Now imagine that instead of these words, I had given you the following instructions:

Check carefully whether each statement is 'true', 'false' or 'don't know'. If you're absolutely sure that a statement is true, mark in the 'true' column. If you're sure it is false, mark in the 'false' column. If there's any doubt about it, don't hesitate to choose the 'don't know' column.

When I've actually given people *these* instructions, they almost always get the exercise entirely right.

5   *The importance of early feedback*
If, as you'd started the exercise, someone had said, 'are you sure there really was a robbery?' – this would have been enough feedback to prevent you from going along the train of thought that there must indeed have been such an event.

6   *The danger of long sentences!*
     Statement '18' is the longest sentence on the list. To remind you of
     it, it is:

18   *The following events were included in the story: someone
     demanded money, a cash register was opened, its contents
     were scooped up, and a man dashed out of the store.*

When we look at it carefully, three bits are true: someone *did*
demand money; a cash register *was* opened; and its contents *were*
scooped up. But did a man dash out of the store? All we know is he
sped away. He could have walked, hopped, ambled, or cycled out of
the store for all we know. Yet when *three* parts of the sentence are
true, how easy it is for us to assume that the final part must also be
true. (This is a favourite trick of party politicians who will tell us in
electioneering speeches some concepts that we know are true – then
will slip in the bait – the bit we're meant to swallow. And we do!)
      Now there's another way of dealing with that long sentence of
statement 18: breaking it into its separate components. That
means four things rather than one:

18   *someone demended money*
19   *a cash register was opened*
20   *its contents were scooped up*
21   *a man dashed out of the store*

      Now in that version, just about everyone agrees that 18-20 are
true, but that 21 is 'don't know'. In other words, a long instruction
causes confusion, which does not tend to happen if the same
words exactly are broken down into a series of shorter instructions. Whereas, when the four parts are presented in a single statement, most people 'swallow' the last bit, because the other bits
were patently true.

Other matters arising

You've probably noticed that once you 'twigged' the purpose of the
exercise, you were on a course to cracking it successfully. In other
words, if you started to approach the exercise with the frame of mind,
'now what *don't* I know?', you were assured of getting the right

answers. This is a good way to approach using any set of instructions. Always confront the possibility that there are elements that you have not yet worked out about them.

Don't be afraid to ask other people what they think the instructions really mean. Sometimes the instructions will have been translated from a foreign language in the first place – especially with electronic instruments which have been manufactured in a far corner of the globe. If you find yourself installing a video recorder that has been made in China, don't expect that the instructions will be as simple to follow as you may have found with one made in Birmingham! The machine may well work in exactly the same way, but the words may not be as helpful. Of course, if you come from near Newcastle-upon-Tyne (as I originally do) the Birmingham words may not help much either.

'WIRMI'

An unusual word, to say the least? It stands for 'what it really means is…'. This can be very useful when following instructions. Once you've worked out what an instruction says, put it into your own words. 'What it really means is…' is a good lead-in to the true meaning of most instructions. This helps us to personalize any individual instruction, so that we work out what we are supposed to actually do with it, or in response to it.

The mechanics and thermodynamics of Yorkshire puddings!

The final section of this chapter is just to remind you how good you already are at 'following instructions' – those you've probably entirely forgotten that you ever learned. Also, you may have found your own ways to adapt the instructions to suit your own tastes. I mention Yorkshire puddings – but if you don't like these, or don't make them, you'll be able to think of an activity involving just as many steps and skills. This time, for fun, let's put the instructions in the wrong order! In fact, when we're doing something new, a list of instructions can often seem quite daunting, but when we've already done it a few times, the same list seems really simple. Putting the instructions in the wrong order for something we can already do gives us another chance to see how complex it may actually be – and how easily we mastered it. We can do more, with confidence.

10

TIPS AND WRINKLES | on following instructions

1 Read quickly through the whole list of instructions without doing anything at all – don't panic – you're just finding out how many instructions there are at the moment.

2 Check through the instructions to see what you'll need to have beside you when you start to work through the list (for example, a screwdriver and a hammer when putting together self-assembly furniture).

3 Make sure you've got all the parts that you're supposed to have.

4 Remember that following a set of instructions is simply a matter of doing one thing at a time – not trying to remember all of the instructions all at once.

5 Often instructions are backed up by illustrations or pictures. Take time to study these – it's often easier to see something than to work out what the words in the instructions mean.

6 Start on instructions number 1, and tick it off on the list when you've completed it. (This saves accidentally missing out an instruction sooner or later.)

7 If there's an instruction you can't follow, don't move on to the next one hoping for the best – try to find someone who has done a similar job before – never be afraid to ask for help.

8 Don't expect a set of instructions to be perfect! Many may have been written and printed in a different part of the world by people who aren't too good at your language.

9 Take the attitude that working through a set of instructions is a very useful way of 'learning by doing' – the best way to learn anything.

10 Take pride in your achievements when you've successfully followed a set of instructions! Use your achievements to encourage you to try more things in this way.

Instructions: in jumbled order (some need doing more than once)

- quickly pour the mixture into the tin and pop it straight back into the oven
- turn off the oven
- find an egg
- don't forget it will be very hot!
- if it's stuck to the tin, gently bang the tin on your table or floor
- take a mixing bowl or jug out of the cupboard
- eat it as soon as possible, before it gets cold
- measure out seven fluid ounces of milk into the jug or bowl
- turn out finished Yorkshire pudding onto a plate, and divide into portions
- crack the egg into the water in the jug or bowl
- stirring vigorously all the time, gradually add the mix
- take a cupful of plain flour
- add a little cooking oil or fat to the tin
- place it in the hot oven for a few minutes, till the fat or oil is hot and smoky
- pour yourself a small glass of the kitchen sherry
- add a pinch of salt to it now if you like it that way
- get a towel, cloth or oven glove ready
- if it looks just as you like it, take it out of the oven
- find the plain flour
- when the time is about right, check the colour
- if you like gravy with it, make some now
- if you drop it on the floor and no-one noticed, don't say anything
- choose a tin of a suitable size
- mix it quite vigorously
- turn the oven on, and set it at about 230°C

Warning: the author and publisher of this book absolve themselves from any responsibility for anything unfortunate that could result from anyone trying to follow the set of instructions given above.

Be a lateral thinker

Let's think again about using equipment, mechanical objects, tools and machines of any sort. When you have a go at using something you've not tried before, it's quite natural to be a little preoccupied with the thing you're trying to do. However, all sorts of other useful and interesting things can accompany your efforts.

For example, learning to use a stills camera is not just about finding out which button to press when, or which sort of film to use, or how steady to hold the camera, or how to get the focus right. The more you experiment with photography, the more you learn about all sorts of other things, such as making photographs original, interesting, creative and memorable. You learn by practising, seeing your results and taking notice of other people's reactions to your results. You find that your skills of observation increase, and you get more pleasure just at watching the world around you with that extra degree of awareness.

If you are learning to use a video camera or camcorder, you also become much more aware of the skills which go into making good television sequences. Only when you've made some really shaky or jumpy sequences yourself do you really start to appreciate all the sophisticated fade-ins and fade-outs which are important parts of good television. This enhances your appreciation when you view films too.

Think back to anything you've done recently that involved using a new machine or tool. Ask yourself 'what *else* did I learn from the experience?'. You may be surprised at how many other things were involved. Not least, you will have learned a little more about yourself – that's always useful.

A problem is only a problem until you know how to solve it. Having to do something new with a tool or machine may feel like a problem. However, once you've done whatever it was and succeeded, it's no longer a problem. It's best to regard problems as opportunities to learn as a great deal of our everyday learning stems from problems we simply have to get on and solve for ourselves. We can learn far more by solving our own problems than by simply getting someone else to solve them for us. When we've overcome a problem, we feel proud and confident and the more we feel like this, the more we feel like tackling new problems.

5

Page fright

Words fail me

Sadly, for many, many people this seems to be true. They feel that their learning failed, and the feeling is associated with words. It may have been the words that did not manage to get them the examination results they wanted. It may have been the words they spoke at an interview that did not get them the job they wanted. We all remember times when we said the wrong thing at the wrong time in the wrong place. We re-live such experiences in our nightmares. We hardly notice, however, all the times when we said the right words, at the right time and in the right place. This does not leave us with any particular feelings – we just move on to say something else.

With written words, at least we may have time to check them. Spoken words can't be erased. We can't wind the clock back and start our sentence again. All this means we may become quite afraid of words – or afraid that we're going to use them wrongly or unwisely.

Lost for words?

Monkeys aren't known for saying too much, nor for writing letters or poems. As the human species evolved, so did our powers of communication. Basically, it means that the noises we make to each other – the symbols we write, or draw, or type – mean something to us and to other people. We try to agree between us a system where the same sounds mean the same thing to most people, and the same symbols give the same message to most people. We make a language. There are many different languages, some of them very different from the one you're reading now. For example, Chinese, Arabic, or Greek look quite different on paper from English, French or German. Most of us have nearly all of our knowledge and skills in one particular language, but it is perfectly possible for human beings to be highly skilled in several languages.

Communicating is such an important part of our civilization that if anyone is 'lost for words' and says nothing or writes nothing for a long time, they are assumed to be *not themselves.* Sometimes we say nothing or write nothing because we are afraid that words will fail us yet again. Yet if we think about it, we learned the meaning (not the spelling yet) of a very significant number of words before we even started to speak. And very young children just starting to speak are not afraid of making mistakes with the sounds of the words they make – they just press on adjusting them gradually on the basis of the effects that are achieved by using them. Babies don't worry about mistakes!

Thinking words

I'd like you to try something next. When you've finished reading this sentence, spend about a count of ten looking at the box below, and just letting your mind think *– about anything at all – but don't do anything with the box just yet.*

Next, jot down in the box what you thought in those few seconds.

Probably you will have noticed two things from what you've just done:

- you thought of a lot more than you could possibly write down in a box of that size; (you know the feeling of 'my whole life passed before me' just before the bus knocked you down?)
- you thought in *words*

You may indeed have thought all sorts of things. You could for example have thought any of the following:

- now what on earth is he going to ask me to do with the box? Last time I saw a box I was asked to write things in it. Shall I look ahead and find out? Or will this be cheating?

10
TIPS AND WRINKLES | on taking risks and learning from mistakes

1 'If a thing's worth doing, it's worth doing badly' – at least at first. Then, it's possible to do it better. (If you wait till you think you're going to do it well, you may never even try.)

2 Try to forget the word 'mistakes' – think of them as research into finding better ways of doing things.

3 It's always worth stopping to work out what went wrong, and how you can avoid that next time.

4 The only mistake is not having a go.

5 The only real risks are ones where people can get hurt – don't take that kind of risk.

6 Most other 'risks' are opportunities to succeed.

7 Think of three ways you can approach learning something. If one turns out to be a mistake, at least you've another two courses of action.

8 Remind yourself that more has been learned from making mistakes than from all the books in the world.

9 'To err is human', to learn from our mistakes divine.

10 Spelling mistakes can be regarded as bold statements of our personal inventiveness!

- how am I supposed to think for a count of ten? If I think about counting, 'ten, nine, eight', and so on, I'll just be thinking about the numbers. And am I supposed to count quickly or slowly? What's going on here?
- well this is very odd. It's the first time I've ever been asked to think for a count of ten, and just looking at a box. Is this supposed to mean something special? Are we going to talk about boxing next, or metal boxes or cardboard boxes, or wooden boxes, or coffins? Very odd...

Almost certainly you thought of something completely different. It's rather strange in a way. As our species evolved, surely our ancestors used to *think* long before they invented words which described what they were thinking about? And we ourselves often think in ways that are just about beyond straightforward words – especially when it comes to feelings, emotions, moods, instincts, and senses. However, we have developed our skills at putting them into words. Many of us at some times in our lives put our strongest feelings into words, in writing, say, love letters, or even letters of complaint!

Finding out

Learning is finding out. Many kinds of learning involve finding out from printed materials such as books, newspapers, magazines, and journals. We gradually improve our skills at finding out from printed words – or handwritten words. We also find out from words in other situations: advertisements on walls, in trains or on vans; words on our television screens; words on computer screens; words on food wrappers, and so on. We don't actually remember very much of all that we see or read in a day – imagine how full of useless information our brains would become. When we're deliberately trying to find something out, however, we actually want to remember some of what we read, and we therefore need to read the words in a rather different way.

We also find out from words we hear of course. Again, we don't make any conscious attempt to learn most of the words we hear. What would be the point of remembering last Tuesday's six-o'clock news? But sometimes we actually do want to remember important things that we hear, and so we either make recordings of them so we can hear them over and over again, or more often we write them down. Writing them down seems to work better for most of us than simply hearing them over and over again.

Living on a planet which is bursting with information, and getting more of it by the second, it's a sensible question to ask: 'How on earth do I find out what to find out?'. That's where the three nuns come in shortly.

Whodunit?

Think of how many detective stories there are around, and television programmes, series, and films where the name of the game is trying to work out, 'who did it?'. This, of course, is also finding out. It's not just 'who did it?' though, it's 'when did they do it?', 'how did they do it?' and 'where did they do it?'. Questions are also posed as to 'why did they do it', 'what happened to them when it was found that they'd done it?' and 'why *was* there a face cloth waving in the breeze like a flag, pinned to the chimney of all places?'. Like monkeys, we are curious animals, but even more curious.

The stranger the situation is, the more we want to find out about it. We want to know. We want to understand. We like finding out. That's why so much of our entertainment is based on the investigative type of situation – detective work.

This urge to find out is something we can harness when we're learning new skills. The more we can regard our learning as a detective story (with us in charge, of course), the more interesting the plot

86

becomes. If we're in charge of finding out from all the words we can lay our hands on (or our ears on?), the words are not nearly so frightening.

'Did I read something about "three nuns" a minute or two ago?', you may be asking. Yes you did – I wanted to stir the detective instinct in you so you'd be ready for them when you meet them – which is right next.

10

TIPS AND WRINKLES | on adventure and discovery

1 Regard every new challange as an adventure, not a problem.

2 The world was discovered by adventurers, not scholars.

3 Discovery is often the act of finding out what is already there.

4 There's always something useful to be learned in any new adventure – even if just not to try it that way next time.

5 Always be on the lookout for things that no-one seems to have noticed – that's sometimes 'discovery'.

6 There is more waiting to be discovered than humankind has discovered so far.

7 'Getting lost' is often the most useful part of any adventure.

8 Everything you learn can be looked at as personal discovery.

9 'Adventures' are things that go well – and things that go not-so-well – and they are all learning experiences.

10 Most discoveries are not made by famous people – but many people who make discoveries become famous.

The Three Nuns

Actually, this bit is about the 'Three Ns' but that's not as easy to visualize somehow. It's a simple principle, in fact. Look at it this way. All the information you will ever meet is in one of three categories: *need-to-know, nice-to-know, nuts-to-know!*

Let's look at each in turn.

Need-to-know

Need-to-know stuff is worth learning. This category includes that which you will need-to-know in your job, in your recreation, in your life in general. If you're studying something formally, the need-to-know category includes all the information which you may have to prove your command over, for instance, in exams or interviews.

There's not usually very much information in the need-to-know category. It's often possible to condense all the most important facts, figures or ideas on a topic into just a few pages of notes. And if we really get to grips with these pages, we can demonstrate that we have a good grasp on the topic. So how do we decide what we need-to-know? We're better able to do this by thinking about the differences between this sort of information and all the rest. Let's explore the rest next.

Sister Need   Sister Nice   Sister Nuts

Nice-to-know

This is a vast category. It's so huge that it's impossible to imagine how big it is. Our universe is full of information that is fascinating. All the libraries on earth contain just a fraction of it. All the television broadcasts on all the channels and satellites are full of nice-to-know information. We are like sponges. We are immersed in this sea of nice-to-know information, and every now and then we take a bit more of it into ourselves (and lose a bit of the information we already had absorbed). A sponge can only hold so much, or it would grow to an enormous size and explode.

So, *most* of the information you will ever meet comes into the nice-to-know category. This is a big problem. That's why I've added a third category – read on!

Nuts-to-know!

This category is almost as big as the nice-to-know one. The nuts-to-know category includes all the information that we don't need to know. It includes all the information that however fascinating, serves us no useful purpose if we try to memorize and store it in our heads. Sadly, students learning for exams often spend far too much of their time learning something that they couldn't possibly be asked in their exams. That's why I first called this the nuts-to-know category.

Examples

- I occasionally need to find the square-root of a number (the square-root of nine is three, the square root of twenty-five is five, but what is the square-root of two? Actually, near-enough it's 1.414. But I don't need to remember this any more – I just use a calculator whenever I need it. I once was taught how to work out longhand the square-root of any number. I think this information belongs to the nuts-to-know category, so I've forgotten it now.

- You may have a card that gives you money from a cash dispenser. This is probably a need-to-know number. I once forgot mine, and after three 'tries' the machine swallowed my card. It took days to get it back. It's not a good idea to write the number down anywhere, where other people may work it out, and treat themselves to some funds from your account. So this is a need-to-know number and I know mine now.

- With nice-to-know information, probably the best idea is simply to know where to find it if and when you need it. That's where books come in. Or card indexes, or diaries, or filofaxes. All those nice-to-know telephone numbers can be stored in such places, and as long as you know where you've put the source of information, you're alright.

But I hate learning from books!

When we're learning something, there's every chance that we'll have books to consult. Many people were put right off books in their schooldays. Books then had to be taken care of, handed back at the end of the year, and were never really ours. We could not write on them and put our own thoughts into them.

One of the problems is that we probably never had the benefit of some really useful advice about how to make use of a book as a learning resource. It's never the case that we have to read a book and commit all of its contents to memory. When we're learning from a book, we've got a much more interesting task to do – and a much less difficult one. All we've got to do is to find out from the book the information that we need to know. We can safely ignore most of the nice-to-know stuff, and are well-advised to be on the lookout for the nuts-to-know stuff too.

The next set of 'tips and wrinkles' looks at a logical approach to going about making use of a book. It's important that we feel that we are in charge of the way we go about using a book. We don't simply have to read the book – we have to use it as a tool in our quest of learning.

Lay an egg!

I'd like to introduce a very useful idea here – one which we'll take further in the next chapter too. The idea is to draw an 'egg' – an oval – in the middle of a piece of paper. About real size (or Size 2 if you're really particular). Then you write in the egg the main idea you're wanting to find out about.

Now if that detective urge is still stirring in you, you may be wondering, 'why an *egg* ?', 'why not just a circle?', 'or a box?'. Well there is an answer, but not the one most people expect. Suppose I'd said,

10

TIPS AND WRINKLES | on finding out from books

1 Work out what you really want to find out from a book or several books. Make a list of the main questions you're looking for answers to.

2 Find the 'right' book in the first place. Library staff are particularly good at helping you to pinpoint the books that will be most useful to you.

3 The most useful books in libraries are often 'well thumbed'. If a book has been borrowed often, the chances are that it's a good one.

4 Look at the contents page of the most promising books, and check which books seem to deal with the topic you want to explore.

5 Look first for books that introduce the topic from basic principles, rather than ones which start at an advanced level.

6 Scan a book by looking at the chapter headings. See how the information in the book is put together.

7 Remind yourself of the things you want to find out from the book, look again at the contents pages, and jot down the chapters and page numbers that seem most relevant.

8 Look at the index of the book and look for key words connected to the things you want to find out. Jot down the page numbers listed beside these words.

9 When you find out the answers to your questions, jot down which page they were on, and in which book (for future reference), and make your own brief notes of the answers.

10 Resist the temptation to 'simply read any book'. It's usually much more important to extract what you need from a book than to try to swallow the whole book!

'draw a circle in the middle of a blank sheet of paper', can you imagine how many people just wouldn't bother, and would skip the task, because they had nothing with them to draw a good circle with? But ask people to draw an egg, and they do just that without thinking. Actually it goes deeper than this too. I like the idea of 'eggs' as the beginnings of creation of life and ideas. I'd like to show you how powerful they can be in helping you to harness your creativity, knowledge and experience.

Suppose you had picked up a book on gardening, and you wanted to find out how to grow chrysanthemums.

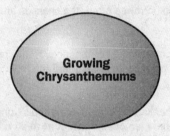

Growing Chrysanthemums

That's our egg with our main idea in it. But there's not enough space round it for what we're going to do next.

The idea is to think of all the questions that you want to find answers to about how to grow chrysanthemums, so that when you consult your gardening book you know what you're looking for.

The next stage of 'laying the egg' is to draw little spokes around it, putting a question at the end of each spoke. I'll give you some spokes – see if you can think of some questions you may want answers to. On page 93 I've put my own attempt at doing this (but of course the questions you will think of are probably much better than mine – I've never grown any chrysanthemums yet!).

Have a go at this next, just for fun.

Put questions you may want to find out the answers to at the end of the spokes round the egg below. Try to use as many spokes as you can – you can add some more if you like too.

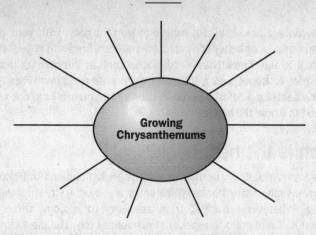

When you've had a go at this, have a look below where I've had a go myself. Don't expect mine to be as good as yours though!

Response to 'lay an egg' on 'Growing Chrysanthemums'

Here's my go at laying the egg. Your questions are probably better than mine, and are bound to be in a different order, but the order does not matter. That's an advantage of 'eggs' – we can let our eyes roam round the points in any order we choose (unlike when we look at a list, where we tend instinctively to go down it).

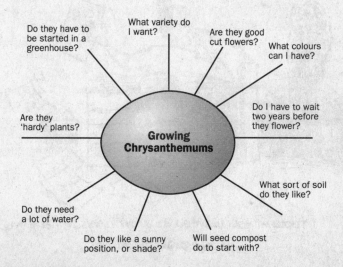

Do you see how useful it can be to go to a book with your own agenda in mind – or better still, your own agenda firmly on paper? It all goes back to the 'Three Nuns' – all books contain information that is merely nice to know, and a lot that's quite nuts to know. When you consult a book for a definite purpose, the clearer you can be about what you need to know the better.

Which is the best book?

This is a very sensible question to ask. In bookshops and in libraries there are usually many books which cover a subject we're thinking of learning. Whatever the topic, from astrology to zoology, there are books on it. There are often specialist magazines too. The most expensive book is by no means always the one that will work best for us. It is indeed hard to tell which to buy or borrow. Here are some clues for your detective work when looking for the best books.

" I thought you wanted to grow chrysanthemums, not draw them ..."

1   *See what other people think of their books*. If you know someone
    else who is learning the same topic, ask them what they really
    think of the various books they've used. Ask which one they
    would keep if they were only allowed to keep one, and which one
    they found gave the most understandable introduction to the sub-
    ject when they first started studying it.

2   *Ask library staff for advice*. Library staff are not only trained in
    how to find which book is best for an individual's needs and
    wishes, they have had a lot of practice at it. They *like* to help peo-
    ple. Don't think of yourself as a nuisance – ask. If you've already
    got a short list of questions you need to find the answers to, this
    will help the librarian find you the right book.

3   *Browse*. You can, of course, browse in bookshops, looking at the
    range of books you may choose from. However, no bookshop will
    have everything, and sometimes the best book may be out of print
    or between editions, and not available at any bookshop. So browse
    in libraries too – no-one will mind you browsing (if you hover too
    long in bookshops you can get the feeling that they're wanting you
    to buy something quite soon).

4   *See what's well thumbed in libraries*. This is often a really useful
    clue. A book that's been used or borrowed a lot is often better than
    ones that spend most of their time on the shelves unused. You
    can't tell this in bookshops where everything is new. Also, if you
    see more than one copy of a book sitting on the shelf in a library,
    that in itself is often a clue that it's a popular book.

5   *Check what the book cover says*. Many books have information
    written by the publishers on the covers (particularly the back
    cover). This often says who the book is aimed at. This can help you
    decide whether the book is at the right level for you, or whether
    you need more detail, or a gentler introduction to the topic.

6   *Look at the 'contents page'*. Doing this will quickly help you see
    whether the book covers the topics you're looking for, especially
    when you've already decided exactly what you want from the book.

7   *Check the index.* A good index can save you a lot of time as you track down the parts of a book you really need to learn from.

8   *See if you like the book.* This seems an obvious thing to suggest, but it matters. If you really like the style of presentation, and the tone of a book, you're going to find it a lot more satisfying to use. We've all got our own tastes when it comes to tone and style.

9   *Use more than one book when you can.* Even if you've found a book that's just right to learn from; it is often useful to look at others now and then. The different approaches usually give us a deeper insight into what we've learned.

10 *Don't get too many books!* It's dangerously easy to get hooked on collecting books, rather than using them. Unless you really want to do profound research into the social habits of lesser-spotted chestnut-warblers, you won't need a shelf full of books on birds. When you've got too many books, most of them will stay shut!

A notorious detective?
(Taking down the evidence!)

However good we are at finding information, the fact that we have it sitting on our shelf or table does not mean that we've learned it. We need to combine our detective work with the accompanying paperwork – that means making notes. We can, of course, just copy out the most important bits from our books, and that is quite useful in that we collect together all the main information in one place. However, copying something out is not a very productive learning activity:

* it's slow
* it can be boring
* we tend not to remember much soon after we've done it

It's a good idea to keep in mind that you're *making* notes, not just *taking* notes. In other words, involve your mind as well as your pen or pencil when you make notes.

One way of making notes is to start with a blank sheet of paper, and begin at the top left-hand corner, and write down important points all the way down to the bottom right-hand corner, then start a new sheet. This means that all of the sheets will soon look very much like each other – and that's *boring*! It's best when each page of our notes looks individual and interesting. There are many ways of making interesting-looking notes. Tony Buzan has given a lot of advice and examples on making 'mind-maps' (or 'spider diagrams'), as a way of consolidating our thinking. (Please see Further Reading on page 176 for titles of some of his books.)

Another way of making notes is to use our 'egg' idea from earlier in this chapter, but this time to record the answers rather than to ask the questions.

Why not have a go at doing this now? You don't even need to go and find a book to make notes from unless you want – you could make some notes from this book. I'm going to make some from Chapter 1, and if you do this too you can compare yours with mine (don't expect them to be the same of course, we all make notes of what we want to remember, and we're all different).

Make some egg notes now!

Make 'egg' notes on Chapter 1 using the following diagram, adding what you think are the most useful points to you at the end of the spokes. (Alternatively, make your own notes on anything else in the same way – but then I can't give you something to compare with your answer.)

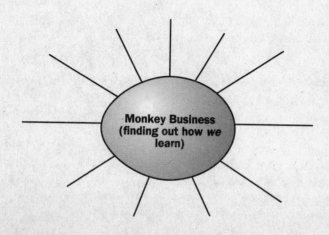

Monkey Business (finding out how *we* learn)

Response to note-making exercise on ideas from Chapter 1

This is my attempt to summarize the main ideas from Chapter 1 in the form of an egg diagram.

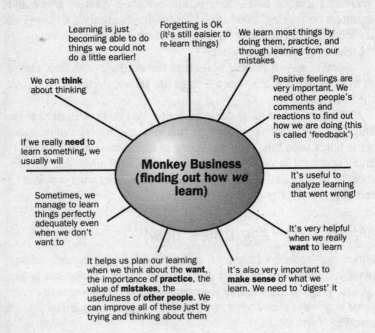

Learning is just becoming able to do things we could not do a little earlier!

Forgetting is OK (it's still eaisier to re-learn things)

We learn most things by doing them, practice, and through learning from our mistakes

We can **think** about thinking

Positive feelings are very important. We need other people's comments and reactions to find out how we are doing (this is called 'feedback')

If we really **need** to learn something, we usually will

Monkey Business (finding out how *we* learn)

It's useful to analyze learning that went wrong!

Sometimes, we manage to learn things perfectly adequately even when we don't want to

It's very helpful when we really **want** to learn

It helps us plan our learning when we think about the **want**, the importance of **practice**, the value of **mistakes**, the usefulness of **other people**. We can improve all of these just by trying and thinking about them

It's also very important to **make sense** of what we learn. We need to 'digest' it

10

TIPS AND WRINKLES | on research and note-making

1 There's nothing mysterious about research – it's simply 'planned finding out' or 'intentional discovery'.

2 If you know what you're looking for, you're more likely to find it.

3 Work out the questions for which you're seeking answers. Armed with a list of questions, your research will be more efficient and productive.

4 When you find out the answers to your questions, or other useful information, capture it – write it down.

5 Don't just take notes, copying things down. Make notes – put things in your own words in your own way.

6 Make your own note-maps – spread out key words or ideas right across the page and put boxes or rings round important ones, and draw lines connecting linked ideas.

7 Within a day or two of making some notes, look at them again and mentally fill in the details behind your notes.

8 Carry some of your notes around with you, and look at them during the odd few minutes every now and then that would otherwise be wasted – sitting in a waiting room, standing in a queue, waiting for the kettle to boil.

9 Make your notes colourful. Maybe use a different colour for really important things. If your notes look interesting and attractive, you're more likely to keep looking at them again.

10 Write questions in your notes. This helps you to be looking for the answers as you learn more about the topic.

6

Taming paper tigers!

My sheet's gone blank!

The last chapter was mainly about finding information and catching it. This one is mainly about getting to grips with it, expressing it, and giving it back – taming it, in other words! We'll look at what we need to do when putting something in writing. Tasks involving writing come in many forms and include:

- writing letters to friends and relatives
- writing formal letters to offices, authorities, shops, MPs
- writing reports
- writing essays
- writing poetry, drama, scripts or sketches, even writing for radio or television
- writing a personal diary or log
- writing notes to other members of the household

In the last chapter, we dealt with the research and investigation which may often precede the act of writing something. Now we're going to look at putting information down on paper.

The one element that all the above have in common is the starting point – a blank sheet of paper! For many people, a blank sheet of paper is a challenge. We can sit and look at it for minutes, without ever moving a pen or pencil. When we really get into it, we can look at a blank sheet for *hours* without putting a mark on it. We can even put the sheet in a safe place until tomorrow, next week or next month!

There's nothing new in this. Many people who have written several books know it as *blank sheet fright*. It's as though now that we're set up to start to write something, all our thoughts just evaporate. Actually,

10

TIPS AND WRINKLES | on starting on a blank page

1 Write 'first thoughts' or 'first draft' at the top of the page. This helps to avoid aiming for perfection in your early attempts to fill the page.

2 If you find that a full sheet of paper is still quite hard to start writing on, tear it in halves or quarters – these are much easier to start writing on!

3 Don't aim to start at the beginning straightaway. It's often much easier to jot down ideas 'in the middle' of the thing you're writing about, and then work both ways, towards the beginning and towards the end.

4 Don't be ashamed of your terrible handwriting! No reader of this book has handwriting worse than mine!

5 It's often quite useful to write on several different sheets of paper at once, giving each sheet a heading, and putting ideas on the sheets relating to the various headings.

6 Leave plenty of space for second-thoughts and third-thoughts in your early attempts at writing something. Don't just fill the pages from the top-left-hand-corner towards the bottom-right-hand-corner in the way that you might have been taught to do at school.

7 Squeeze new ideas into suitable space on whichever page is most relevant. New ideas are always valuable, and keep coming up all the time you're writing something (and even after you've finished).

8 Don't be afraid to cross out old ideas when you think of better ones. Even if your draft pages start to look very untidy, it's better to keep developing and improving your ideas than just to stick to the first ones you had.

9 When you've got enough 'draft pages' with sufficient 'draft ideas' on them, spread them out in front of you, and decide what the most logical order is to reassemble them.

10 Start now on a new blank sheet, and write your 'second draft', linking together the ideas in a sensible and flowing way. Remember, you can have as many drafts as you wish before you declare your work 'finished'.

the problem is often more like too many thoughts being in our minds, and we find it difficult to know where to start.

It's useful to remember the 'Three Nuns' we met earlier. If we're writing anything, the importance of the 'need-to-know' category of information is as strong as ever, and there's no use wasting our energy writing about the 'nuts-to-know' stuff.

Feelings about essays

Most people returning to learn have some apprehension about the inevitable task of writing essays. Many people have bad memories associated with writing essays in their schooldays (or 'compositions' as some of us remember them being called).

Part of the problem may have been that blank sheet fright. Another problem was that it may have felt uncomfortable to put our best thoughts down on paper, hand them in to be marked, get them back some time later covered with red ink, and with our spelling mistakes all underlined, and so on. This was our feedback. This is how we got other people's comments. And we learn so much from other people's comments – yet few of us remember positive feelings associated with getting

"Are your essays always as fluid as this?"

our marked essays back.

Part of the problem was red ink! Even green ink would have had less damaging effects. Can you remember the feelings that red comments gave you? And most of the comments seemed to be about the things we did incorrectly, with only the odd '✓' when we did something well! It would have been much better if we had got our essays back covered with *positive* feedback, with phrases such as:

excellent point

quite so

I agree with this

that's a good idea

you're absolutely right here

that was a good way of putting it

a good, solid conclusion; well done

One thing that may have solved many of our bad experiences about writing essays would be if someone had actually showed us how to do it. Well, I suppose they did try, but they tended to show us how completed essays might appear, rather than how to actually go about writing one ourselves. I'm going to try and write one now, and would like you to join me on my journey.

I am trying to do several tasks at once here, so please be patient. I would like to:

- suggest a way you can go about writing any essay you need to in future, especially those which may count as 'assessed coursework' in your future learning
- talk you through the process by giving examples as we go
- give you a 'first draft' which was done by following the steps in our discussion

Let's write an essay!

Let's write an essay on the title 'How to Write an Essay'! I'm going to try to show you *how* I do this (and how I wrote this book in fact). I'll do it in a set of lettered steps (from 'A' to 'Q'; don't panic, big tasks are done in one easy step at a time). Then I'll add my comments about each step (with a bit of fun thrown in!). Finally, I'll try to write this essay myself – you do it too if you like, and compare notes with me.

A   Take a blank sheet of paper

'Well, that's obvious isn't it?'. 'And you write the title of the essay at the top of the page?' No, I don't do that yet. Guess what I do?

B   Draw an egg in the middle of the page. Put the title in that

You may have seen from Chapter 5 how useful the 'egg' technique can be for collecting together questions, and for collecting information in our researches. It's even more useful for writing essays (and books). Here goes.

Notice that I use the sheet 'the wrong way round' – or landscape rather than portrait. That's straightaway got over the problem of blank sheet fright – in seconds. There's egg on my page, and the title – but nothing else yet.

C   Next, I start thinking and drawing spokes

It does not matter at all about the order of my thoughts – I'm going to leave that till later. I simply want to get my thoughts down quickly. Let's get that blank sheet filled up. This isn't going to be the essay itself, of course.

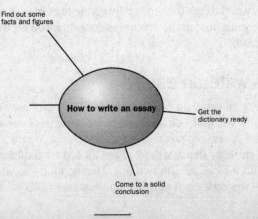

That's my first few ideas jotted down. The page looks much less blank already!

D   Continue ...

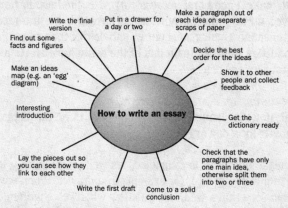

Now we're getting somewhere. All sorts of ideas, but not in any particular order yet.

E   Sit back and think for a while
Are there any points missing? Are there any that are not important? Let's assume that this time there's nothing more to add.

F   Number the ideas; '1' for the first thing to do, and so on
This isn't as hard as you may think. Here goes...

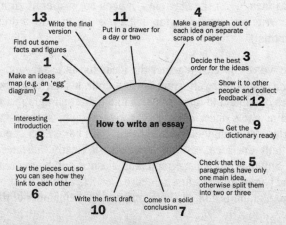

Of course, this is not the only order that these steps can be done. But it is a start. Notice that I leave writing the introduction till quite near the end? This is because the introduction is very important – it needs to create a good impression for the reader. (There's no second chance to make a good first impression!) Also, the introduction needs to 'be lived up to' - the essay needs to go where the introduction is pointing towards. There's no better way to do this than to save writing the introduction until the main bits of the essay have all been written and the conclusions reached.

G   Start turning an idea into a paragraph

I'll try this now, for example, with idea number 11 on the diagram. 'Put it in a drawer for a day or two.'

11: When the first draft is completed, it's well worth putting it out of sight for a day or two, for example in a drawer. When we've just written something, we think we know what we've written. In fact, we know what we think we've written – which may be rather different! Putting an essay out of sight for a day or two gives us the chance to read it more objectively. When we come back to it after some time, we can see what we have actually written, and often we can make all sorts of little adjustments and improvements, making the final version much better than it would have been.

H   Continue turning ideas into paragraphs, preferably on separate pieces of paper

(This was idea '4' on the diagram – it does not matter at all in which order we write our draft paragraphs. I'll now try to write a draft paragraph on this!)

4: Once we've collected together the ideas for an essay, and decided on the best order to structure the first draft, it's useful to take small pieces of paper and turn each idea into a draft paragraph. We don't need a whole sheet of paper for a paragraph, so half-sheets or quarter-sheets may do perfectly well. Each paragraph should contain only one idea. It's best if the idea is clearly indicated by the first sentence of the paragraph, and 'fleshed out' by the remainder of the paragraph. The first sentence then lets the reader know what the paragraph is going to be about, and the remainder of the paragraph gives the reader the information that has been led up to by the first sentence.

I   Check that paragraphs have only one main idea in them otherwise split them into two or three
(That was step '5' on the diagram. Look above to the paragraph I wrote for '4'. In fact, there are two ideas there, so that would be better as two separate paragraphs as follows.)

4:    Once we've collected together the ideas for an essay and decided on the best order to structure the first draft, it's useful to take small pieces of paper and turn each idea into a draft paragraph. We don't need a whole sheet of paper for a paragraph, so half-sheets or quarter-sheets may do perfectly well.

5:    Each paragraph should contain only one idea. It's best if the idea is clearly indicated by the first sentence of the paragraph, and 'fleshed out' by the remainder of the paragraph. The first sentence then lets the reader know what the paragraph is going to be about, and the remainder of the paragraph gives the reader the information that has been led up to by the first sentence.

J   Lay the paragraphs out so you can see how they link to each other
This helps us to check that we really have got them in a sensible order, and that one leads smoothly into the next. At this stage, we may often decide to add a new linking paragraph between two of the ones we've already written. Also at this stage, we may decide that we have the odd paragraph that does not really help – ditch it or recompose it.

K   Come to some solid conclusions
Most essays ask us to decide something, or review something, or conclude something. Now that we've got all of our paragraphs drafted, we can look back at the title, and decide what the final conclusion should be.

L   Write an interesting introduction
I've already explained why it's best to do this after you know what's going to be in the essay.

M   Get the dictionary ready
This will be needed as we compose the first draft.

N Write the first draft

This time, starting at the top of a full-sized blank page, begin with the title, then one-by-one slip in the paragraphs in the order that you've planned, working all the way through to the conclusion. During this first-drafting stage, check on spellings as necessary, and also do a little tidying up of sentences and grammar wherever you notice the need. Avoid, however, deciding to expand on an idea by writing several new paragraphs just because you've thought of something new. If you really want to include new material, go back to your plan, and see if the material really belongs to the essay – or whether it would have simply been running off at a tangent.

O Put it in a drawer for a day or two

(You've already seen my reasons for suggesting this.)

P Show it to other people and collect feedback

In several parts of this book I've stressed how useful it is to get other people's reactions to our activities. Writing essays is no exception. The other people don't have to be experts in the topic you're writing about. Almost anyone can give useful feedback. You will still have control of which particular bits of feedback are important enough to go about making substantial changes, and which simply suggest minor 'tweaking' of the first draft.

Q Write the final version

This is it! If you're working on a word-processor, you can usually write the final version quite quickly just by assembling various bits and pieces you've already done, with the changes and improvements added in as you go. If you're writing the essay longhand, it usually does mean starting with one further blank piece of paper! However, this time you're simply transcribing material that you've already compiled, so there's no blank sheet fright around. It is now time for your most readable handwriting.

Don't be surprised, though, if by now the first draft you're transcribing from is looking really messy with crossings-out, pencilled additions, asterisks and footnotes, and so on. This means you've made a good job going from first draft to the final version. Of course, you can make second, third and twelfth drafts before you get to the final version. Many parts of this book had five or more drafts before they reached the stage you see.

Well, after all that, let's put it to the test. Now I'll try to do it

My first draft

In what follows, I've used exactly the approach we've just been exploring to write an essay on writing essays! If you're tired of reading about writing essays, and itching to write one yourself on something entirely different, please do.

During the process, I followed the 'egg' diagram that you saw earlier, though in the first draft below, you may notice that sometimes I added an extra 'linking paragraph', and occasionally absorbed one idea into a paragraph reflecting a further idea.

As you may remember, I did not suggest that the final essay would have the ideas in the 'egg' diagram in numerical order all the time – for example, the introduction is not written first.

To help you link the paragraphs in my first draft below to the 'egg' diagram, let's repeat the diagram here, and add numbers – in round brackets e.g. (3) – to the essay to show you which paragraphs reflect which step in the plan. I've also used square brackets, for example [8] to show where the actual introduction and conclusion of the essay itself are. (Of course in a real essay these numbers would not be shown!) Let's suppose the instruction I am to follow is this:

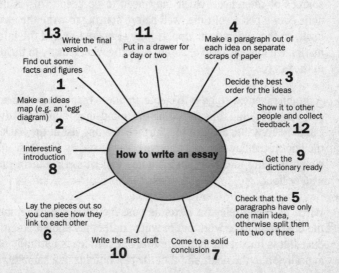

Task: write (in approximately 1000 words) an essay on 'How to Write an Essay'.

How to Write an Essay

[8]   Writing essays is an important skill needed by people in schools and colleges and also by adults returning to education, and training in mid-career and beyond. Assessed coursework in many subjects takes the form of essays marked by tutors. Many examinations require candidates to write essays 'against the clock'. The purpose of this particular essay is to describe a logical, and step-by-step approach, which helps people to develop their skills at writing essays. Though the approach to writing essays discussed below is not appropriate to writing essays under exam conditions, practising this approach leads to much greater skill and confidence when tackling essays in exams.

(1)   The first stage is to conduct any necessary research. The most important thing to do first is ensure we know exactly what the title or task is meant to be, allowing us to decide the information we wish to seek out. This means finding out facts and figures, which may need to be included in the essay, and details of other sources of reference, which may need to be cited. This is best done over a period of time, well before starting to write the essay itself, so that we have an opportunity to make sense of the information we have available, before deciding what exactly to include in the essay.

(2)   A productive next stage is to create an 'ideas map'. There are several ways of doing this, including the 'mind-map' approach advocated by Tony Buzan (see the Further Reading list at the back of the book), the 'lay-an-egg' approach suggested by Phil Race, and simply writing ideas on post-it notes and clustering them on a wall or floor.

(3)   When as many relevant ideas as possible have been identified, the next stage is to work out in which order they should be introduced. It is important to ensure that one idea leads naturally and logically on to the next, and that the plot unfolds in a smooth and

coherent way as the essay continues. Starting with the ideas map, a useful way of deciding what the best order is consists of putting numbers against the ideas as we decide where to start, and where to go next, and so on.

(4) Once we've collected together the ideas for an essay, and decided on the best order to structure the first draft, it's useful to take small pieces of paper, and turn each idea into a draft paragraph. We don't need a whole sheet of paper for a paragraph, so half-sheets or quarter-sheets may do perfectly well.

(5) Each paragraph should only contain one idea. It's best if the idea is clearly indicated by the first sentence of the paragraph, and 'fleshed out' by the remainder of the paragraph. The first sentence then lets the reader know what the paragraph is going to be about, and the remainder of the paragraph gives the reader the information that has been led up to by the first sentence.

(6) Having assembled a number of paragraphs on separate pieces of paper, it is useful to lay them out so they can all be seen at once, in sequence, and to check through to see that the flow is smooth and coherent. At this stage, it may be necessary to add further paragraphs to 'bridge gaps' between one idea and the next.

(7) Next, it is useful to move straight on to thinking about how the essay will conclude. A good ending is the hallmark of a good essay (and a good thriller or novel too). When an essay is being assessed, the ending can be particularly important as it is likely to be the last part that the examiner reads before beginning to make decisions about the score or grade.

(extra!) When deciding how to conclude an essay, it pays dividends to look hard once more at the essay title. In particular, if the title is in the form of an instruction, containing words such as 'discuss', 'outline', 'describe', 'give advantages and drawbacks of...', 'analyze' and so on, the conclusion needs to address words of this sort very directly. If, for example, the instruction included the word 'decide...', the conclusion needs to be a decision.

(8) The next thing needed is a good introduction. It is worth leaving this till now, as the best time to write a convincing introduction is when we know two things: what we are going to introduce, and what our conclusions are going to be. A further reason for writing the introduction after most of the ideas have been drafted is that the wording and impact of the introduction are particularly important. The introduction is the first thing that any assessor will see, and a good introduction may create favourable first impressions, which will endure well into the essay itself.

(extra!) An introduction can often work well by answering two questions: 'why?' is the topic covered by the essay important, and 'how?' will the essay aim to address the topic. This gives a sense of purpose to the essay, and also an idea of how the essay will be structured to address the purpose.

(10(9)) By now, all the main parts of the essay will be in the form of draft ideas and sentences, on separate pieces of paper. The next stage is to write the first draft of the whole essay (with a dictionary at the ready). This is now quite straightforward as it is simply a matter of linking the ideas together in the order that has already been decided.

(11) A useful next-step is to put the completed first draft out of sight for a day or two, then come back and read it afresh. It is surprising what we see after that day or two, that we would never have seen if we had tried to read the essay immediately after finishing writing it. When we have just written something, we see what we meant to write, not necessarily what we actually wrote.

(12) It can also be very useful to show the first draft to other people. Friends, colleagues, fellow learners, partners – anyone's feedback is valuable. Other people's reactions to our work can often alert us to further things which we could have included, and to what is unclear or ambiguous.

(13) At last, the final draft may be written. In practice, it is sometimes useful to go through several drafts if time and circumstances allow before putting together the final version.

[7]   As can be seen from the discussion given above, writing an essay is a complex task, but one which can be broken down into a series of straightforward operations which in themselves are quite simple. The discussion here has not included that of tone or style – these important issues would require a further essay to do them justice. Following the sequence suggested in this essay should enable people, who have not in the past regarded themselves as skilled at writing essays, to put together excellent examples.

How did I do? 1159 words in fact – just a little longwinded, Phil! When there is a suggested word limit, it's best to try to be within 10-20 per cent of it. If you write an essay twice as long as asked for you'd be likely to lose some marks – and if you only wrote one half as long as asked for, you'd probably not get too many marks anyway.

Don't forget there would not be numbers beside paragraphs in a normal essay – I put them there simply to help you see how the paragraphs related to the mind-map diagram that we explored earlier.

How well am I learning?

Question banks are a very effective way of monitoring for yourself how your learning is going. Even when you're just learning for the sheer satisfaction of finding out something new, it's good to know how well you're learning it. It's even more important to monitor your learning when preparing yourself for any assessment, or examination, you may be heading for.

Question banks are lists of questions you collect to practise with. When you're going in for an exam, you're going to be sitting and writing down the answers to the questions on the exam paper. It's never too early to start practising answering questions. Exams measure how practised you are at writing down answers to questions. If you've often answered similar questions before the exam, your speed will be good and you'll not have to think too hard to answer the questions in the exam itself.

However, there's no need to wait until you can get your hands on some old exam papers before you start practising answering questions. Make your own! The best questions are short, sharp ones. Even a long complex exam question is really just a few short questions rolled into one. The sort of questions to put in a question bank are usually one-liners. Here are some nonsense ones to give you the idea of the kind of questions I'm getting at!

What's a grunge widget?
State 'The Law of Lompicality'
Who first discovered bungjam?
How does a flugelmotor work?
When would you notice kerplonking?
Why does parbling happen?

(If you happen to know answers to these questions, I'm rather worried about you!) How do you decide which questions to include in your question bank? It's actually straightforward. You simply look at your books, your notes and any other learning materials you're using, and ask yourself:
'What may I be expected to become able to do?'

It's useful to add one more word to this question to ask yourself:
'What may I reasonably be expected to become able to do?'
You then simply look at your notes and decide – one thing at a time – what you may be expected to be able to do in due course. It does not matter if you can't yet do many of these tasks – writing down the questions is at least half-way towards becoming able to do them.

Sometimes, from one page of a book or your notes, you may be able to think of a dozen or more short, sharp questions to add to your question bank. When you become able (through practice) to answer these questions at any time, you'll know everything you need to about that page and will be able to answer anything about it that could reasonably be asked of you.

Example of a question bank
Let's suppose you were going to have a test on 'How to Write an Essay'. Suppose you'd been given this chapter to read, and rather than having to write an essay yourself, you were going to be asked questions about how you should approach writing essays. In other words, suppose you were trying to learn what we said earlier in this chapter about essays. Your question bank could look something like this:

1 What's an essay?
2 What's an 'egg' diagram?
3 Why is an 'egg' diagram useful in sorting out ideas for an essay?
4 Why is it worth saving the introduction till last?
5 How many different ideas should be contained in a good paragraph?
6 When should the conclusions be written?
7 What should be done just before writing the first draft?
8 Why should it be put in a drawer for a day or two?
9 Should I show the first draft to other people and, if so, to whom?
10 Why is the introduction particularly important?
11 Why is it important to have a firm conclusion?
12 When am I most likely to need to write essays?

If you look back to what we said about essays earlier in this chapter, you could probably double the number of questions and you will be able to think of better ones than those above. Notice that I numbered the questions, but the order does not matter. When you're studying a large topic, the number of questions you can practise with may run into several hundreds, and even thousands. That's why it's worth numbering them.

Another reason for numbering your questions is that you can make an 'answers bank' to go with your 'question bank'. When you're stuck for the answer to a question, you can then simply look it up in your 'answers bank'. Let's make an 'answers bank' for those twelve questions next.

Answers Bank

1 A longish piece of writing, usually as the answer to a question, either written in an exam, or as part of assessed coursework.

2 A way of making a mind-map of ideas, where the central topic or question is written in an 'egg' in the middle of a sheet of paper, and one idea at a time is written at the end of spokes radiating out from the 'egg'.

3 It helps us to generate lots of ideas and helps us to see them all at once, so that we can make sensible decisions about the order in which to use the ideas when writing the essay.

4   Because only when the rest of the essay has been drafted do we really know what the introduction is leading in to.

5   Only one. The first sentence should make it clear what the paragraph is going to be about, and the rest of the paragraph should add further details or explanations.

6   As soon as all the 'ideas paragraphs' have been drafted, but before writing the introduction.

7   Lay out the separate bits of paper with the various ideas for paragraphs, and check that they lead smoothly one-to-the-next, adding in any extra bits needed to make them flow well.

8   So that I can have a fresh look at it, and notice any changes I need to make, or any rough edges that need attending to.

9   Yes, just about anyone can give useful comments.

10 Because it's the first thing that will be read, and first impressions are important.

11 Because most essay questions ask for something quite definite to be done during the essay, and a firm conclusion reminds anyone marking it that this definite thing has indeed been done.

12 When studying something involving written assessment, such as exams or tests, or coursework marked by tutors.

Of course, what you see above are not the only ways that the twelve questions could be answered, but they give a good enough idea of how to answer the questions for practice purposes.

More about designing and using question banks

Formats

There are several ways to build up your collection of questions and answers. These include:

- a pocket notebook with the numbered questions starting at the front of the book and the corresponding answers starting from the back of the book. This format is handy to carry around, which means you can practise with your question bank at almost any time – for example, while travelling on trains or buses, or in odd moments between tasks at home or at work.

- a 'card index' box which you can get in a variety of sizes containing cards in a selection of colours. If you use small cards, you may decide to write only one or two questions on each card with the answers on the other side of the card.

  This sort of question bank gives you the chance to pick cards at random – or shuffle the pack - so that you gain practice at answering your questions in any order rather than the fixed order of a book-type question bank.

- if you're handy with computers, you can design your questions and answers on the screen, and can even program the computer to fire questions at random at you – and even keep a score of the number you get right.

Ways of using your question bank

Experiment for yourself. See what helps you most in your learning. Possibilities include:

- When you've only got a short time, select a page (or card), and simply scan the questions, pencilling a '✓' beside those you know you can answer without looking anything up, an '✗' besides those that you know you can't answer at present, and a '?' beside those that you're not sure whether or not you can answer just now. Simply finding out what you can't yet answer is a very useful process. You can find out quite a lot of this in the odd few minutes between jobs.

- Gradually use your question bank to find out which particular questions cause you most difficulty. When you know exactly what the difficult bits are, you can focus your attention on them regularly until they become easy.

- When you can, get someone else to quiz you with your question bank. It doesn't have to be someone who knows the subject you're learning – they've got the answer bank too, so they can tell whether you're giving reasonable answers.

10
TIPS AND WRINKLES | on questioning

1 If you don't have any questions, you won't find any answers.

2 Every piece of knowledge is just the answer to a question.

3 Keep asking 'why?'. There are interesting reasons behind everything that is important.

4 Keep asking 'who?'. All learning involves people in some way – sometimes the answer to 'who?' will be 'you'.

5 Keep asking 'what?'. The unknown becomes the known when you know what it is.

6 Keep asking 'when?'. Knowing 'when' is as important as knowing 'why', and 'what'.

7 Keep asking 'how?'. When you know how, what, why and when, you will know everything about something.

8 Ask people 'what do you really mean?', when you don't understand what they tell you. They'll probably be able to explain themselves better then.

9 When you're learning something new, write down as many questions about it as you can before you start. You'll notice the answers all the more when you already know the questions.

10 There is no such thing as a silly question. There are, however, silly answers. Questions are more important than answers.

- Keep adding to your question bank. Spend a few minutes, every day if possible, thinking of a few extra questions that you're going to become able to answer when needed. Your question bank can cover everything in the 'need-to-know' category for what you're learning.

My memory just isn't what it used to be!

How often we've said this. However, it is well known that we have much better memories than we give ourselves credit for. We only use a small percentage of the brainpower that it is possible for us to harness. We remember a lot more than we ever give ourselves credit for. Under hypnosis, people have been found to remember things that they did not know they could remember! The problem is not so much about what we can remember, but about what we can recall. 'Getting it back' is the important part of memory – in particular getting it back just at the moment we really want it or need it.

Brains don't like to be forced!

How often have you had something 'on the tip of your tongue'. It was there in your mind one instant, then just as you wanted to pull it to the front of your mind and use it – it was gone again. And try as we might to force our brains to bring back these memories that were almost there – they seem to go further and further away. In fact, the harder we try to force our brains to deliver the missing information, the more our brains seem to rebel, and deny us our wishes. Students in exams often get 'mental blanks' when they desperately try to force their minds to deliver some information. The harder they try, the more their minds rebel, until they temporarily refuse to deliver anything at all – a mental blank!

The solution to this problem is quite simple – we need to make ourselves ways of getting our brains to recall things that we may need. This is most successfully done by using various kinds of 'memory by association' techniques. This usually means linking some important information with something quite different – but easy to remember. Even better, if we can have a mental picture of a situation, and then decode that situation to extract the information we require, we become able to recall things even under the tense conditions of exams.

"Now I remember what I wanted to ask you... do you fancy another drink?"

Hooks and hangers

That's where practising answering questions is a really useful thing to do. The more often we've practised answering a question, the more easy it is for us to remember the last time we did it, and the time before, and so on. If I answer a question correctly today, then refresh my memory enough to do the same tomorrow, then have another look at it next week twice, then once a week thereafter for a month – I'll almost certainly never forget it! And the time it takes to refresh the memory gets less. I may have to spend five minutes today, but it may only take me two minutes tomorrow, and next week half-a-minute may be all it takes to remind myself about it. In the next month, I may just have to think for a second or two, and the whole picture will pop up in my mind. In short, learning things often helps us learn things well.

10

TIPS AND WRINKLES | on improving concentration

1 Don't think that everyone but you has a magic power of concentration. There's nothing magic about concentration – you can do it as well as anyone else.

2 Don't try to concentrate on hundreds of things at once. Concentration is about thinking of one thing at a time.

3 Work out exactly what you want to know – write it down in the form of questions. You can then concentrate on them one at a time and find out the answers.

4 Making your own notes helps you to concentrate. This also helps you to think of one thing at a time.

5 Don't expect to concentrate for hours on end. Concentration spans last seconds rather than hours!

6 When we're really interested in something, or fascinated by it, we tend to concentrate automatically. Try to become fascinated by what you're learning!

7 Concentrating on something once is rarely enough. Make time to go back and remind yourself of things that you've already learned. Difficult ideas need several spells of concentration before we grasp them fully.

8 Try to make sure that the things you try to concentrate on are the important things, not the background details.

9 When you've been trying to concentrate on something for a while, have a break. Your subconscious mind will carry on sorting out what you've been concentrating on.

10 If you find yourself struggling to concentrate on something, take a deep breath, and let it out, feel your body relax – and you will concentrate better.

Make your own hooks and hangers – mnemonics

'Mnemonics' (pronounced nem-on-iks) is an odd-looking word for something we've all used.

Think of the following five letters:

E   G   B   D   F

What do they mean to you? Jot down in the box any special signif-icance these letters have for you – and (if they have), how you remem-ber that significance.

Musical mnemonics?

Many people remember these letters through a little phrase they learned years ago at school. This may have been 'every good boy deserves favours', or 'every good boy deserves fruit' or 'every green bus drives fast'. Any of these gives the letters E G B D F in the right order, simply by noting the first letters of the words. The special signif-icance you may have remembered is that they are the names of the lines on the treble clef in music. Even if you'd forgotten that, the chances are that you still remembered one of the little phrases.

That's what mnemonics do. They are ways of using something that's easier to remember to help us to recall something that's harder to remember.

Colourful mnemonics?

Let's look at another one. You may remember being taught the colours in a rainbow (or in the spectrum of the sun's light). These colours have a 'right order' when we look at them in order of increasing wavelength. This is:

red orange yellow green blue indigo violet

In the next box, either see if you can remember a way of getting these in the right order, or invent a little sentence of your own that helps you to do this.

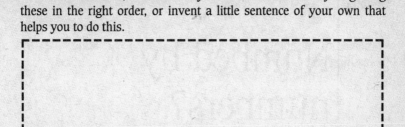

Many people remember a little sentence that helped them get these in the right order – 'Richard of York gave battle in vain'. I remember this myself, and can use the first letters of the respective words to get the colours. There are not many other colours beginning with 'r' than 'red' and so on. I can't remember anything at all about who Richard of York was, or about what battle he did not win – but that does not matter.

You may, of course, have invented a sentence of your own to write in the box. Here are another two that I've just invented!

'Reach out your glove bending in vans'
'Reading out your gardening books is violent!'

Those aren't somehow as memorable as 'Richard of York' – but at least we can get a mental picture of either of these odd sentences, and if we practise recalling the words and linking them to the picture once or twice, we've got it.

Number mnemonics?

Next, I'm going to teach you a number. It's the one that has the Greek letter 'pi' (which looks like this: π). We'll learn it to eight figures!

The number is: 3.1415827

Go on – learn it!

Now here is a very easy way to learn it.

Think of the little sentence 'how I wish I could remember pi quickly'. Count the letters in each word – 3,1,4,1,5,8,2,7. The sentence is easy to remember, and using it we can get π back anytime we wish!

7

Numbed by numbers?

$$2\{3x + 4y\} \int f(x)dx \geq 0$$

Well, I think that's nonsense – so only be numbed by it if you think you understand it!

Of all the topics under the sun that seem to have given humankind headaches, none is more pervading than 'sums'. Mathematics, we call it sometimes. And it has it's special facets like algebra, geometry, trigonometry, arithmetic (this one's really just 'sums' and all that). Many of us didn't like any of these when we were at school, couldn't do any of them well, were told we were bad at them, and that we were hopeless. The one thing we really learned well was the last in that list – we were hopeless, always will be (we think), and have what's called a 'mental block' about numbers.

Count Dracula?

Numbers basically are about counting. Not too sinister yet. But the horrors get worse. If ever we manage to conquer arithmetic, algebra, geometry and trigonometry, there are a whole set of harder things to give us worse headaches. These include differential calculus, integral calculus, Boolean algebra (where it definitely doesn't add up, I believe), and Heisenberg's 'Uncertainty Principle' (which apparently means that if the train is exactly on time, it will not be going to where you thought it was). (Actually, I should be fairer to Heisenberg, he worked out that if you know exactly where, for example, an electron is, you don't know how fast it's moving, and if you know exactly how fast it's moving, you don't know exactly where it is. This is true, the only problem being that no-one quite agrees about exactly what an electron is in the first place.)

Dracula was a vampire, and they bite. This is not to be confused

with 'byte' which in computer language is a single item of information. Computers handle lots of bytes at a time, and we talk about megabytes. The little machine I'm writing this on has a 'hard disk' (so I'm told) which can contain forty megabytes of information at once (that for me is more books than I'll ever write), and my smaller portable has even more with eighty megabytes (but its batteries only last on the train from Cardiff to Burton-on-Trent, and are flat long before Edinburgh).

But back to vampires. Many people believe their maths teachers were vampires, and also find that their bite was even worse than their bark. Such people suffer the symptoms of having become 'Numbed by Numbers'. (However, really good mathematicians are usually very nice people, and often really talented musically, and it is known that their Bach is at least as good as their Byte.)

How do you figure?

'Figures' are the problem for many of us. It's almost a foreign language. We can *read* words, we can *speak* words, but we can't do either of these with numbers. As soon as we see a number, the dreadful truth strikes us – we're expected to do some *thinking* about what it means, and are probably required to add it to some other figure, or subtract something from it, or multiply it by something else, or do a bit of 'long division' on it, or find its square root – it gets worse and worse.

Actually, it's not nearly so bad as it seems. Working with numbers is just like anything else when we get down to how we learn it. We learn it by doing it. In particular, we learn it by not getting it right first time – or second time – then finding out why. We need feedback when we're learning to work with numbers. It's no use just telling us what the 'right answer' is – we need to know why we didn't get the right answer when we tried it ourselves.

And what if we did manage to get the right answer, but by a route that is different from the so-called 'right' way of solving the problem? Are we wrong if we get the right answer by the 'wrong' method? The only 'wrong' we may be guilty of is that of taking a longer way round than necessary as we can all see the value of finding and using the shorter routes. In essence, that's what skill with numbers is all about – being able to get the right answer to a problem as effortlessly as possible. Now why didn't those vampires tell us just this?

Can I use my calculator?

More and more, in examinations testing people's skills with numbers, calculators are not only allowed, they're expected. This is a positive step forward compared to the old days when examinations in this area essentially measured people's skills at arithmetic, rather than their real grasp of numbers. A much more valuable skill in real life is that of making a *'good guess'*. This can be called the skill of 'estimating'. Or can we call it 'guesstimating'? Let's take a simplistic example, as follows:

Which is the nearest answer to: 3 x 3 = ?
(a)   1
(b)   10
(c)   100

Now we all know that 3 x 3 = 9. Therefore the nearest of the options above is 10, not 1 nor 100. Despite the simplicity of this example, the skill involved is very important. To overcome any 'numbness' with numbers, we need to have a *feel* for them. (Numbness is lack of feeling!). We need to know instinctively whether the answer that our calculators give us is approximately 'right'. As with anything else, the skill is developed by practice, and particularly by trial and error. Have a try now at the following questions.

Question 1
Which option is the nearest to the answer for the addition sum below?

100 + 10 000 + 92 =   (a)   10 100
                                          (b)   11 000
                                          (c)   10 200

Question 2
Which option is the nearest to the answer for the following multiplication sum?

450 x 1.35 =   (a)   6 000
                                   (b)   600
                                   (c)   60

How did you get on?
1   *The correct answer is 10 192, so which of the three options was best?*
(a) Not bad, but still some way out.
(b) No, a long way out – there weren't any 'thousands'
(c) This is the closest: 10 192 and 10 200 are almost the same (you could say £101.92 and £102.00 are only eight pence out – not much to worry about in a hundred pounds).

2   *450 x 1.35 = 607.5 in fact*
(a) 6 000   no, this is nearly ten times bigger than the correct answer.
(b)   600   yes, this is near enough for a 'guesstimate'.
(c)   60   no – but you didn't choose this one now did you?

These little examples were only to give you the idea.

Exercise: calculator versus brain!

Do this now if you can lay your hands on a calculator, or save it for when you can use one.

The idea is to think of some 'sums' of your own, then make a 'guesstimate', then (and only then), use your calculator to work out the actual answer, and see whether your 'guesstimate' was reasonably close. I'll give you a sum to start off with in each case, and then you think of four more on your own.

Addition sum	'your guesstimate'	the actual answer	was it near?
(1) 465 + 78 =?			
(2) + =?			
(3) + =?			
(4) + =?			
(5) + =?			
Subtraction sum			
(6) 843 – 456 =?			
(7) – =?			
(8) – =?			
(9) – =?			
(10) – =?			
Multiplication sum			
(11) 35 x 87 =?			
(12) x =?			
(13) x =?			
(14) x =?			
(15) x =?			
Division sum			
(16) 703 ÷ 41 =?			
(17) ÷ =?			
(18) ÷ =?			
(19) ÷ =?			
(20) ÷ =?			

The power of being approximately right!

When you've done the preceding exercise, you may have surprised yourself in three ways:

- most of your 'guesstimates' were probably quite close to the real answers
- you found you got quicker at making 'guesstimates'
- you actually found yourself enjoying playing with numbers

Of course, you don't have to stop now, simply because this exercise is over. If you're enjoying it, you can get a blank piece of paper and sit there 'guesstimating' for hours. By doing this, you'll be doing something valuable – taking the sting out of Count Dracula's bite.

Being approximately right with numbers pays dividends. For example, if you can make a reasonable 'guesstimate', you will be able to know at once when:

- your shopping bill is quite unreasonable, because there has been an error in entering £10.50 instead of £1.05 for an item
- you're adding up the bills for a month, and you accidentally add up the gas bill at £350 instead of £35
- you've bought twelve cans of something at eighty pence, and are wondering whether a £10 note will be enough or not
- you're charged eight per cent interest per year on a loan of £3 000 towards a new car, and wonder how much interest you're going to pay over three years
- you've won a £2 bet on a horse at 25-1, and wonder approximately how much you'll actually get

It is also very useful when shopping to be able to keep a mental tally on what's gone into the basket or trolley. The trick is to round everything up or down to the nearest pound and add them up as you go. If something is £4.80, simply count it as £5.00. If something else is £3.15, simply call it £3.00. If something is £1.50 it's better to call it £2.00 than to call it £1.00! Make a game of it. Keep adding up the approximate score as you fill your basket or trolley, but only in round numbers – think pounds and not pence. If you've added a bit on to the last item by rounding it up, subtract a bit from another item by rounding it down. Just before you get to the checkout, tot up your mental

" I bet you'd be amazed to know that I'd already worked out what this would add up to, to the nearest 60 pence!"

score (write it down on a scrap of paper if you can). Then compare your 'guesstimate' with the actual till receipt. You will find that you can become really quite good at knowing how much you're spending every time you reach for something on the shelves.

Keeping your cool!

What's the weather like today? Somewhere in your reply is bound to be something about how warm it is or how cool it is. And even when just thinking about this, it's probable you have a rough idea of what temperatures you're thinking about.

Just for starters, jot down in the box below what you think the temperature is where you are at the moment (probably indoors), and outside the building in the shade.

The temperature today	
Indoors	Outdoors
°C	°F
°F	°C

Remember degrees Fahrenheit and degrees Celsius (or Centigrade – both terms have been used)?

I wonder if you entered the indoor and outdoor temperatures in both kinds of unit? You probably remember being taught at school how to convert one to the other. Many people found this confusing, and forgot it with relish as soon as they did not need it any more.

Just to refresh your memory, the two scales are as follows:

The Celsius, or Centigrade, scale takes 0°C as the melting point of ice, and 100°C as the boiling point of water, at sea level (water boils at a much cooler temperature up Everest).

The Fahrenheit scale takes 32°F as the melting point of ice, and 212°F as the boiling point of water, at sea level.

So the difference between the boiling point of water and the melting point of ice is 100°C or 180°F.

Remember better weather?

Years ago, everyone talked about a hot day as 'in the seventies', or a very hot day as 'up in the eighties' and a raw wintry day as 'only in the lower forties' and a brass monkeys day as 'down in the twenties' – all talking of course of the approximate Fahrenheit temperature. For a long time now, weather forecasts have mentioned Celsius temperatures, and sometimes thrown in 'that's sixty-five degrees Fahrenheit' for good measure. Most people agree that the weather is better in Fahrenheit than in Celsius (though for scientists and engineers the Celsius scale makes a lot more sense for some very good reasons).

How to go from Celsius to Fahrenheit

For anyone for whom this was a pain, I'd like to show you that it is actually quite easy. Now the way you probably remembered it from school was:

'Multiply the Celsius temperature by nine, divide it by five and add thirty-two'

This is true, of course, but it does not exactly stay in our brains.

Whether the weather is hot?

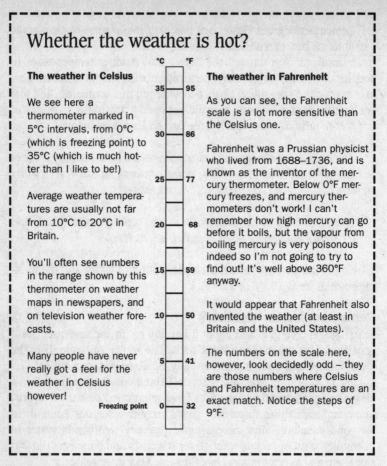

The weather in Celsius

We see here a thermometer marked in 5°C intervals, from 0°C (which is freezing point) to 35°C (which is much hotter than I like to be!)

Average weather temperatures are usually not far from 10°C to 20°C in Britain.

You'll often see numbers in the range shown by this thermometer on weather maps in newspapers, and on television weather forecasts.

Many people have never really got a feel for the weather in Celsius however!

The weather in Fahrenheit

As you can see, the Fahrenheit scale is a lot more sensitive than the Celsius one.

Fahrenheit was a Prussian physicist who lived from 1688–1736, and is known as the inventor of the mercury thermometer. Below 0°F mercury freezes, and mercury thermometers don't work! I can't remember how high mercury can go before it boils, but the vapour from boiling mercury is very poisonous indeed so I'm not going to try to find out! It's well above 360°F anyway.

It would appear that Fahrenheit also invented the weather (at least in Britain and the United States).

The numbers on the scale here, however, look decidedly odd – they are those numbers where Celsius and Fahrenheit temperatures are an exact match. Notice the steps of 9°F.

Guestimates are still OK!

However, we don't have to do exact calculations to change our weather from Celsius to Fahrenheit – a degree or two either way isn't going to scorch the tomatoes (and only people who have a degree or two in maths or science are likely to notice the difference!)

We've already seen that 0°C is the same as 32°F (melting ice). Now, for every extra 5°C we go up, it works out that the weather gets warmer by 9°F. So, 5°C is 32 + 9 = 41°F. And 10°C is 41 + 9 = 50°F, and so on.

Look at the diagram, and you can see the scale on the left going up in multiples of five, and that on the right going up in multiples of nine.

For practical purposes, these are the only temperatures we need to know in a temperate climate. Some are particularly easy to remember, as follows:

> 10°C = 50°F is easy to remember (that's pretty cool!)
> 35°C = 95°F is easy too (that's very hot!)

Notice that the numbers I chose to show on the diagram are all whole numbers. Other numbers are not quite so round.

For example, if we try to work out what 23°C is in Fahrenheit, we get:

> 23 x 9 = 207
> 207 ÷ 5 = 41.4
> 41.4 + 32 = 73.4

However, that's less than half-a-degree Fahrenheit above 73°F.

So, we can nearly say that 23°C = 73°F - another one that's easy to remember, they both end in '3'.

How about going backwards from Fahrenheit to Celsius? (Yes, it did seem like a backwards step when they did that to the weather!)

The sequence is just this:

- subtract thirty-two from the Fahrenheit temperature
- divide what's left by nine
- multiply what you get by five

Let's try this with 100°F (your body temperature when you've got a bug!):

- 100 – 32 = 68
- 68 ÷ 9 = 7.5555555555555555555
- well, we don't need all those '5's, so let's just call it 7.5
- 7.5 x 5 = 37.5

So, 100°F = 37.5°C very nearly.

It's all in the blood?

It is possible to measure temperature very, very accurately. In science laboratories, instruments called Beckmann Thermometers can be used to measure even the tiniest changes in temperature. In this sort of work, exact temperature differences matter a lot.

The human body stays at about the same temperature. It used to be about 98.4°F, which is near enough 37°C.

There are special thermometers called 'clinical thermometers' which are designed to measure temperatures in the normal blood temperature range quite accurately. When we say we're ill, someone usually sticks one of these under our tongues (or in places best left to the imagination) and leaves us for what seems like half an hour, then comes back, looks at the thermometer very knowingly, and gives a sad shake of the head (which does not make us feel better at all).

Anyone can buy a clinical thermometer at the chemist. It is very useful to have your own, as you can then be ill as often as you wish. Particularly after having a cup of tea, you will find that you are dangerously ill. If you've been out in the garden on a cold day, the thermometer will tell you that you've already died. Clinical thermometers are such fun – the only day your temperature is exactly what it's supposed to be, you're probably actually quite poorly. It is much more dramatic to be ill in Fahrenheit than in Celsius. 'Temperature of a hundred and two' sounds much more convincing than 'just a bit under 39'.

How low can you go?

It's a long story, but the answer is just a fraction lower than *minus* 273°C. At –273°C everything stops. Not just the trains, but the movement of the components of atoms themselves. Quite sensibly, –273°C is called 'Absolute Zero'. It is a state of zero energy – a bit more dramatic than Monday mornings. However, who heard of zero being the same as –273, you may ask? Well, scientists use the *Kelvin* scale of temperature, which starts at $0 K$ and goes up as high as they want. This means just adding 273 (and a tiny bit) to all the Celsius temperatures we've already thought about. It also means that your sitting room is likely to be something like 298 K, and your blood temperature a shocking 310 K.

Absolute zero is close to the temperature in deep interstellar space (where nothing is moving apart from 'The Enterprise', so we are led to believe). However, in real life, the Kelvin scale will never catch on. Imagine a weather forecast saying that it will be hot and humid in the South East with temperatures of 299 K, while offshore breezes in the

West will keep temperatures down to a mere 291 K. Not much use for the weather, Kelvin.

Scientists and physicists find however that putting temperatures in 'Kelvins' allows them to do many calculations much more easily than if they were to stick to Celsius (and ones that Fahrenheit just would not have dreamed possible).

Hot numbers in the kitchen

°C °F

Hotting things up!

If you think more about cooking than about the weather, you may be more interested in how Celsius and Fahrenheit temperatures compare in your oven.

This time, we've shown only the 50°C intervals, with the Fahrenheit temperatures opposite them.

Some of these are quite easy to remember approximately. For example, 100°C is not that far away from 200°F.

150°C is almost the same as 300°F.

200°C is nearly the same as 400°F.

250°C is not too far from 500°C.

So far as cookers are concerned, we can just about say that the temperature in Fahrenheit is about twice the number in Celsius.

I just don't know, however, how this compares to gas marks!

250 — 482

Hot and smoky: Yorkshire puddings?

200 — 392 Pretty hot: pizzas?

150 — 302 Fairly slow roast?

100 — 212 Gentle braising for a long time?

50 — 122 Warming plates?

Notice this time that when the Celsius temperatures go up in 50s, the Fahrenheit ones go up in 90s. It's the same difference.

0 — 32

Put your head in the freezer?

The same principles work for low temperatures.

However, it does get a bit complicated if we just think about the numbers. (These are numbers that really do numb us physically or mentally – especially if we keep our head in the freezer for too long!)

As you can see, for every 5°C we go below zero, the Fahrenheit temperature falls by 9°F (just as before).

However, the Fahrenheit temperature is still 32°F at the temperature of melting ice, or 0°C.

So we've got to go all the way past -15°C before the Fahrenheit temperature reaches 0°F.

We can see by following the 5s and 9s that -20°C is equivalent to -4°F and below that everything is minus!

If you really like sums, you'll be able to work out that eventually the Fahrenheit temperature catches up with the Celsius one as we go yet further down. There is one very, very cold temperature way down below the scale here where they are the same number. If you can work this out, you're not numbed by numbers. If you can, please write it on a postcard (but don't send it to me, I've just worked it out for myself!).

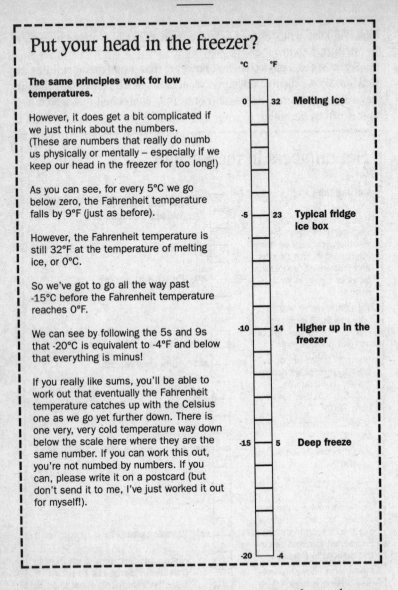

°C	°F	
0	32	**Melting ice**
-5	23	**Typical fridge ice box**
-10	14	**Higher up in the freezer**
-15	5	**Deep freeze**
-20	-4	

Now you know what to expect when you see a '–5' on the weather map. This means '–5°C' of course, and means a fairly sharp frost, with the likelihood of icy patches on untreated roads. (If it had meant '–5°F', the temperature would have been very low indeed – Siberian winter or polar regions get to low temperatures like this, and it would have been below '–20°C'.) At temperatures as low as these, even salt won't keep roads from freezing. However at really low temperatures, ice doesn't melt under our feet or the tyres of our car in the way it does at less-severe temperatures, and ice would be relatively safe to walk on or drive on. I'm not going to try this, I'm afraid – when I put my head in the freezer it's not for long!

Numbed by teachers?

You may be wondering why I've saved my main section on getting the most from your teachers until here in a chapter about numbers? This is because for many people, the teachers they remember with least joy or affection were their maths teachers at school. Why on earth was this? Let's see what you remember of your teachers – particularly those who tried to teach you to handle numbers.

How did you feel about maths teachers?

Tick as many of the options below that apply to your mental picture of your maths teacher at school.

❏ They were really nasty people, who made me feel inadequate and stupid.

❏ They were very strange people, who seemed to live in a world of their own.

❏ They just didn't have any fun in them – they took it all very seriously.

❏ However hard I tried, I just couldn't understand what they were getting at.

❏ The teachers were alright, it was just the subject. I hated it!

❏ They were wonderful people, and really helped me to love the subject.

The world would be a happier place if everyone ticked the last of the options above, and there would not be any need for a chapter called 'Numbed by Numbers'. However, even if you ticked all of the other options, let's do a bit of analysis on why you may have less-positive feelings about maths teachers. There are very few teachers who are nasty – but it is possible (as we all remember) for us to feel inadequate and stupid, especially in subjects where there are right and wrong answers – and we always seem to get the wrong ones.

It is possible for us to find that some teachers seem to live in a world of their own, especially when for one reason or another we don't seem able to step into their world. If we had problems with numbers, that could seem to us like an alien world.

When we get things wrong (or can't do them at all and don't know why) it is not surprising that there seems a lack of fun somewhere along the line.

In fact, the problem is more to do with our feelings about number-subjects than about the people who tried to teach us. However, there is much we can learn about how best to make the most of teachers. Let's explore this next.

Teachers and pupils – what's the difference?

They're both human beings, after all. But the teacher-pupil relationship has often been a somewhat strained and artificial one, especially when we found the subjects difficult.

Teachers can already do something we can't yet do

There's nothing sinister about this. As we've seen earlier in this book, it's perfectly natural to be 'not yet able' – or 'uncompetent'. This is a normal part of becoming able to do something. However, when we get down to our feelings, we can sometimes be in awe of someone who can do things we can't yet do. It would be wonderful if we could just sit back and admire their skills – but we're more likely to cringe and worry about our own lack of ability.

It all seemed to be negative feedback!

With a subject involving calculations and right answers, there's not a lot that teachers could say about how well we did when we got it right. They could hardly say 'you did that sum really well, with a very well organized approach' – we had to be content with just getting it right. However, when we got things wrong, teachers would probe and look

10

TIPS AND WRINKLES

on getting inspiration from teachers

1 When you get a really inspiring teacher, make the most of it. Let such teachers fire up your want to learn.

2 Don't expect all teachers to be inspiring. You can still learn a lot from someone who does not inspire you. Concentrate on the subject at such times; not the person teaching it.

3 You'll get more from teachers if they can see that you're interested. Let your interest show on your face. Have some questions of your own ready to confirm that you're interested.

4 Don't expect to be taught – expect to learn actively. The most you should expect from a teacher is help with the way you go about your learning.

5 Regard teachers as 'expert witnesses'. Be prepared to cross-examine them (nicely) to learn more about a subject.

6 When you don't understand what a teacher is saying, let it show on your face. If you sit there looking alert, alive and interested at such times, teachers will assume you're understanding everything.

7 If you can't follow something a teacher says, there is every chance that many other people are in the same boat. Don't take it as something wrong with your brain!

8 Remember that most of your real learning is not directly from people like teachers but from practice, making mistakes and getting feedback on your own efforts.

9 Don't forget that teachers are human beings, with emotions, feelings, strengths and weaknesses. You'll get more benefit from them if you treat them humanely.

10 Try your hand at teaching. Teach anyone you can something you're good at. This helps you see how teaching and learning work together.

deep into our way of working, and show us exactly where we first strayed from the straight and narrow correct pathway. If we look at it logically, that was exactly what we needed. We benefit from knowing why we're not yet right. But it did not feel good, especially at school, and so many people have less-than-affectionate memories of their maths teachers.

Teachers were old, set-in-their-ways and formal

At school, teachers were older than us. So were our parents. All these older people seemed intent on keeping us in order. They did not seem to understand how our minds worked, or what our interests were. So when an 'older person' tried to explain to us how to do something we could not yet do for ourselves, we seemed to feel that we were being corrected, or disciplined, or rebuked. These feelings often became barriers in our learning.

It always seemed so public and competitive

There was always a 'smart Aleck' who got the answer right and earned praise from the teacher. For the rest of us, when we got it wrong, everyone knew. Our humiliations were public. Even when a patient teacher tried to explain to us individually why we'd made a mistake, the smarting from the public failing was still with us, and got in the way of our chance to learn from feedback.

There was never time to really make sense of it all

As soon as we had managed to master one thing, teachers always seemed to be rushing on to get us to master something more difficult. We rarely had the joy of simply practising what we had already mastered.

So what's changed?

Are teachers now magically different? If we return to try to learn something again which we never managed before, are we going to meet a new type of teacher, full of charm and tact, and with wonderful abilities to help us to understand?

Or have we ourselves changed, maybe on the basis of years of experience of the real world of work, or bringing up a family, or surviving in the supermarket? In fact, it's we that have changed most. School is probably not the best place to learn, and we learn far more when we're in the real world anyway. Suppose, however, that we got back 'to school', maybe to a college or an evening class. Some of the old bad feelings and emotions will naturally try to re-emerge, but now there's a lot we can do to rationalize them.

Teachers are quite human!

When we return to learning as adults, it's often a wonderful surprise to find out how much we actually *like* our teachers or tutors. Often, they are not years older than us. In fact, they may be much younger than us. They've experienced all sorts of events in life that we've experienced. There is a great deal of common ground. We feel we can talk to them as equals.

It's now OK for them to know more than us – about some things.

This is not least because there are all sorts of things that we know that our teachers don't now. There are all sorts of things we can now do for them. Members of an adult class may between them be able to make a wedding cake for the big day of the teacher's daughter, repair their teacher's ailing car, plumb in a new central heating system for the teacher, or simply bake something delicious to pass round to everyone in the coffee break. 'An apple for the teacher?' – much more than this. Teachers of adult classes often really get to know their 'pupils' – they may become friends for life – even marriage partners!

The emphasis is now on how best we can use our teachers

That's what every good teacher wants. Teachers really do want to be able to help people learn new skills – that's why good teachers become teachers. When we return to learn as adults, gone are the days when all the teacher seemed to do was to try and keep the class in some sort of order.

Most of the formality has gone

True, in colleges there are still formal lectures, which have many of the bad old ingredients of the sorts of classes at school that we'd rather forget. However, adult education evening classes often adjourn after class to the local pub and that's often when the real learning happens.

It's back to how we learn naturally – we learn from other people's feedback to our efforts and ideas.

And what about fellow learners?

At school if we could not understand something and asked the pupil closest to us to explain it, we tended to risk, 'Shut up, Jones! If you know more about this than anyone else, tell all of us – otherwise listen and get on with your work!' When we return to learning as adults, we're treated a great deal differently. If we do the same thing, and ask our neighbour in a class, 'What on earth is he talking about?' a sensitive tutor will be quick to help us. 'Ah, Phil, am I right in thinking this bit is hard to understand right now?', 'Let's look at it from another angle next'.

Cheating or collaboration?

Somehow, many of us seem to have been 'trained' at school to work privately and in isolation. Anything else was considered cheating. Yet all the way through this book, we've seen how important feedback is as a natural part of how we learn. Most important of all, we need feedback from fellow learners who themselves are tackling the same things as we are. In most adult education or training courses, tutors and instructors make excellent use of feedback from learners to each other. Every now and then, they will set tasks for *groups* to try – not individuals. Each time, there will be someone in the group who knows a little more about how to approach the task, and the other members of the group benefit from watching their colleague tackle the task.

'Your greatest resource is each other'

I say these words often to college students. I encourage them to make full use of their chances to learn from each other – and in particular to use each other as sources of feedback. I suggest that they organize themselves into little informal 'study groups', and set aside some time each week where the group will meet, with the main item on the agenda being to help each other with matters no one can understand yet. Someone who has just learned it is the best person to explain it to others. This is particularly true of anything to do with numbers, maths or algebra.

10

TIPS AND WRINKLES | on number-crunching

1 Don't worry that pages full of numbers look like a foreign language to you – they are a foreign language but one we can all learn if we do it step by step.

2 Forget all the times you've been told that you were dense just because you weren't good at your multiplication tables. Calculators are very inexpensive now, and much quicker than most brains.

3 Erase from your memory all the pain and boredom of rote learning (reciting tables and so on) at school. We learn to handle numbers by actually doing it, not reciting things about it.

4 As soon as you've found out how to do a particular kind of sum or problem, invent half a dozen very similar ones of your own and do two more today, then one a day for four days. This will help you remember the sequence.

5 Remind yourself how good you already are with numbers – for example, most people can count their change in shops, and thousands of 'non-mathematical' people are really good at working out how much a bet has just won them, or planning which three scores they want from a dartboard.

6 Practice 'guesstimating' – for example, keep a rough check of how much you've spent as you fill a supermarket trolley, until you become good at working out approximately what the cost will be.

7 When you can't understand how to do something with numbers, try to get three different people to explain it to you. Ask them to make you do it yourself, rather than telling you how to do it.

8 Remember that the best persons to explain something to you are people who have only recently learned it themselves. They can still remember how they learned it.

9 There are often several ways to get the right answer. None of them is wrong, but some of them are quicker. Stick to the way that you like best (after exploring any other possibilities that you're alerted to).

10 However complicated a numerical operation is, it's easy when you know how to do it. A problem is only a problem till you know what the answer is.

'Don't tell me how to do it – make me do it, please!'

We can say this to a fellow learner much more freely than to a teacher. When we need help with something involving numbers, there is no quicker way than to get someone who can already do it to give us a driving lesson. Driving instructors don't sit for ages talking about how we should drive – they make us do it and give us help and feedback. The same applies to conquering numbers. Fellow learners can be the best people to give us this help.

8

Mind your language!

'How's your grammar?' 'Not bad at all for eighty-four, really, thanks.'

At school, many moons ago, I learned French and, in due course, I passed the exam. I had passed 'O' level French. Many years later I went to France, and discovered that while I could actually *speak* French well enough to be understood, I could not *listen* to French well enough to understand what I was being told. I have not gone back since. This hurt. I was made to feel particularly silly – think of it – someone who can speak a language really quite well, and ask questions in the language – but who could not understand the answers when people replied to the questions. I've been to Germany, and Egypt, where everyone seems to speak English better than I can speak their languages. I can speak just enough Arabic to say 'thank you' and this helps a lot.

There's another strange thing about grammar. When we first learned our own language, we did not know much about grammar. Think how well many a five-year-old can communicate – they're very good at letting us know what they want – often in no uncertain terms. Yet it will be some years before they hear of grammar. Yet when we start to learn a new language as adults, we seem to find a lot of grammar – that which we never had a second thought about in our own language. In fact, I think I learned more about English grammar from my attempts to learn French and German than I ever learned in English classes. In our native language, the grammar exists – but perhaps we just don't 'mind' it. It can actually be a lot of fun finding out about grammar; we know, but don't know we know!

Nowadays, you can buy machines which will display translated words and phrases to help you make yourself understood in a foreign country. But this is not the same as actually *learning* to use their languages, in ways that let you communicate with people naturally and clearly. Looking back, the problem with my French is that I was taught to have a good knowledge of French *grammar* but not of French as a language. So the first question to ask is 'what do you want to *do* with the language? Do you want to understand how it works, or do you want simply to put it to use? Surely, the sensible answer is the latter. Why else have a language, other than to use it to communicate with people? But perhaps there's more to language than words and rules. Where's the pleasure of language? Let's explore this further next.

Pleasure and pain?

There are all sorts of feelings we can have about languages. You may simply want to use a new language for practical purposes like holidays abroad, or to communicate with someone you know in particular from another country. However, many people really *love* languages for a variety of reasons that are special to them including:

- loving the rhyming and metre of poetry, and the powerful images and emotions that poetry can capture, and the special ways that different languages lend themselves to different imagery and sounds;

- enjoying the skilful use of words in plays and drama, where the written word is specifically intended to become a spoken word, with tone of voice, emphasis, passion or calmness, and the whole range of emotions from pleasure to pain;
- exploring the use of words for fun – comedy, puns, word-play, jokes; there are ways that words can give fun from their appearance on the page, and ways that the fun can only be communicated when the words are spoken, and ways that the fun lies in the words sounding like something other than they appear (puns, for example);
- finding out the subtle differences between languages (the French have many more ways of describing love and passion than the British – and the French language is better equipped for describing subtleties of food and taste as well);
- enjoying grammar! Yes, many people find the rules and structures of different languages absolutely fascinating in their own right.

We have feelings about our own language, and feelings about any further languages we may have learned or are trying to learn now. These feelings may be quite different for the different languages in our lives.

Next, I invite you to explore your own feelings about your own language, and any other language you've learned or are learning. In the quiz that follows, probe your own pleasure or pain with languages. If you're not learning a second language, simply think of your native one. Alternatively, if you may one day try a new language, you can use the 'other language' column in the quiz which follows to guess what your reactions may be (there is no tax on imagination!).

Why mind your language?

For best results, we want a new language to be more than any of the following:
- some new words we can speak
- some new phrases we can recognize and translate for ourselves
- some new words we can write
- some words we can hear, translate and understand

We really need the new language to do all of the above and, to get inside our mind. Our own native language is already inside our minds.

Quiz on languages: pleasure or pain?

Write in the two languages you'd like to compare (your own language need not be English). Then tick whether the following are a pleasure or a pain.

	Your own language		Another language	
	Pleasure	Pain	Pleasure	Pain
1 Finding new words				
2 Grammar and rules				
3 Learning to say new phrases				
4 poetry and plays				
5 Expressivness				
6 Reading newspapers				
7 Reading magazines				
8 Reading novels or romances				
9 Reading texbooks or manuals				
10 Being read aloud to				
11 Reading aloud to someone else				
12 Reading aloud in public (speeches, etc.)				
13 Listening to broadcasts				
14 Listening to people talking to you				
15 Conversing with other people				
16 Writing letters				
17 Writing reports				
18 Writing stories				
19 Writing poetry				
20 Writing plays or sketches				

When we speak sentences, we don't consciously think about what is the subject, which words are nouns and which are adjectives, what tense the verb is in, and whether there are any conditional adverbial clauses, and we certainly don't bother to work out whether we are 'saying' a comma, a colon, a semicolon or a full stop. Nor usually do we bother to think about grammar when we write sentences, except that we do usually put in the odd comma and full stop. Many people don't know the difference between adjectives, verbs, nouns, adverbs, prepositions, propositions, and conjunctions – *yet they communicate really well* with other people, both in writing, and in speech. This is because they 'mind their language' – they are able to express their thoughts in a way in which other people get the meaning straightaway. Surely this is the first aim of mastering any language. If we happen to also become knowledgeable about the grammar, all the better – and if we really enjoy finding out how the language works, and how poetry and drama work best in it, splendid. However, if all we need to do is to communicate reasonably well, and can learn to do this without knowing all the rules, what do the rules matter?

The most important thing when learning a new language is to get a feel for it. This is best done exactly the same ways as we got a feel long ago for our own native language:

- by hearing a lot of it, and gradually understanding more of what we hear
- by trying to get messages across in it (the first word my son learned – and used with emphasis – was 'no!')
- by trial and error – we learn equally well from both
- by gradually becoming better at understanding words we read
- by gradually becoming able to write things ourselves

When we become really interested in a new language, we may want to deepen our feel for it, by a little at a time getting the culture of the country and its inhabitants into our minds. When we understand more of people and their views and ways, we find we understand their language better. When we find out about the differences between their ways and ours, the differences between their words and ours are much easier to take in.

The word's out?

If we pick up a dictionary (one in any language) we see thousands of words. Even in our own language, we see words we did not know existed. It can be fun to take a dictionary, find three completely new words (new to us, that is), then try to use them in something we say or write that day. I've learned many words that way. However, when we pick up a dictionary in our own language, we don't suddenly become frightened by the number of words it contains. We don't have to learn them all. We don't have to understand them all.

Most of us, in our day-to-day lives, don't need to use a vast number of words; we can get by with quite a small number of words. Furthermore, we can often get by with quite simple words rather than long complicated ones. And we still manage to ring up the plumber to fix a leak, to ask for the right ticket at the station, to write a note to the milkman for an extra pint, to order our round at the pub, to arrange a date and time with friends, to ask someone out to dinner, to ask for what we want from a menu, to express our undying affection to our partner or loved ones, to talk to God (or whoever we believe in, if anyone) when we ask in prayer, and to complain to perfect strangers about how bad the weather is! That's what language is all about – communicating with our fellow human bèings, getting what we need or want, and simply getting on with our day-to-day lives.

So how did we learn this? How did we get a grip on the language we know best?

- we *wanted* to learn it, so we could understand and be understood – and not least so we could get our own way when we wanted to
- we learned it by *doing* it – by practising, and learning from our mistakes
- we learned by finding out from *other people* whether we were doing it well enough
- we added each new experience of trying to do it to our ever-growing feel for the language – in other words, we gradually 'made sense' of it all

This is how we 'mind our language' – and exactly the same processes work just as well when we decide we want to 'mind another language' as well.

Laughs and lapses

There's nothing new about learning by our mistakes – but when it comes to learning a language, the mistakes can be really funny. I can't remember which language has very similar words for 'sheep' and 'orange', but can you see what I mean? When we make a real blunder in a foreign language, people will of course laugh! But at the same time – and much more important – they respect us for *trying*. Then, you will find that people become very helpful indeed, and it matters far less if we make any further mistakes. Laughter is one of the nicest kinds of feedback (ask any comedian, or politician, or professor, who likes making speeches – especially after-dinner!).

Even if people are laughing at something we did not intend them to, if we smile back and laugh with them, there's rarely a problem – the more fun we can have in learning a language, the better our learning is. Imagine going home (or to work) and announcing 'you can have anything you want from me today as long as you ask me in French!' You would have all sorts of interesting things to exercise your skills in translation from anyone who already had some French words!

So which bits of the language should I 'mind' first?

Especially if you're intending to go to the country concerned, and to try using the language, the following sorts of information are useful:

- food (you don't want to starve, do you?)
- transport and travel (you want to be able to get around)
- basic courtesies (you need to know how to say 'hello', 'goodbye', 'see you tomorrow', 'my name's Phil, what's yours?', and yes, 'It's just after quarter to three' when someone asks *you* the time)
- money, travellers cheques, banks, credit cards

Look who's talking!

If we want to become good enough at a new language to be able to communicate with people in it, we've got some talking to do first. It's not sufficient to simply get to know a lot of words when we see them – we need to know them when we hear them – and in particular when we hear ourselves *say* them. There are plenty of ways we can get in some practice at talking. These include:

- *talking to ourselves!* We may get some strange looks when people see us talking to ourselves, especially when in a foreign language, but it does our spoken-language skills a power of good.

- *listen and imitate.* There are discs and cassettes of everyday spoken speech in most languages, and listening is only the first step. The imitating is the important step, and the more often we do it, the better we become at it.

- *listen to yourself!* We can, of course, listen to ourselves while we're talking but that only helps to a degree. Do you know people who say things that you can't imagine they would ever say if only they could hear themselves saying them? With a cassette recorder, however, it's quite easy for us now and again to hear ourselves as others hear us. This is particularly useful if we're learning by listening and imitating. We can then hear whether we actually sound as close as we think we are to what we're trying to sound like.

- *talk to people.* Even if they don't understand the language you're learning, it can still be good to talk it to other people. It helps you become accustomed to seeing other people's expressions as you speak the words.

- *teach someone else.* What helps here is someone who knows a little less about the language than we do. Then, if we can interest them to learn a little from us, we can not only talk the language to them, but also explain how the language works;

- *tell the dog!* If you've got a dog (or can borrow one – you can borrow mine anytime!) you'll know how intelligently dogs will look at you when you speak to them. Dogs will do this for hours if you want them to. They won't criticize your pronunciation. One of the best ways of learning anything is to explain it to people. Explaining it to a dog is every bit as good for us – we still do the same thinking as if we were explaining it to a human being.

How to go about learning a language

Let's suppose you've made the decision – you're definitely going to have a go at learning a new language (or trying again with one you've previously struggled with). We've already explored the importance of feelings – let's now end this chapter with some straightforward practical advice. The following twenty suggestions have been adapted from the ideas of Hilary Morris-Evans of the City of Bath College, an expert in language learning.

1   *Approach it 'little and often'.*
    Ten minutes a day works a lot better than an hour all at once (for example, just before a language class you may be attending).

2   *Listen while relaxed or drowsy.*
    Make some bedtime listening a habit, let the language get into your mind in a natural, relaxed way. When you're advanced enough to do some bedtime reading in the language, even better.

3   *Don't worry about mistakes – babies don't!*
    You don't have to get everything right to get your message across effectively. It's nice to get the tense of verbs right, but when you get it wrong don't worry. , Language teachers like their students to make mistakes – otherwise how would they know where to try to help them improve?

4   *It's a challenge, not a problem.*
    Try to regard the differences between your own language and the new one as fascinating rather than frustrating. Don't imagine that only very clever people can speak more than one language fluently – in many countries it's part of the culture that most people know two or three languages. You can too.

5   *Forget what you may have heard about a language being 'difficult'.*
    For example, if you're learning Japanese, is not difficult to learn to speak it effectively – for example, there aren't any verb endings to worry about. Of course it's more difficult to write, but all you may need to do could be to speak it reasonably well.

6   *Don't think you have to crack everything.*
    Don't regard learning a language as a puzzle where you have to master each successive step before you go on to the next. Remind yourself of how you learned your own language – a bit at a time – just enough to get by at each stage.

7   *Feel free to exaggerate the accent!*
Don't be frightened to make strange sounds! Play with putting your mouth and tongue into positions that seem strange or even silly. Remember that there are all sorts of cultural differences which affect the way we make sounds when we speak. For example, the French don't like to say the 'th' sound because it's against their culture to stick their tongues out. Similarly, we don't like to say a 'u' sound in the way the French do as in 'la rue' because it's not part of our culture to purse our lips and stick them forward. Try pursing your lips outwards (in private) and listening to yourself saying '*Oooh*, I wish *you* would *glue* my *shoe*'! (One way of doing this even better is on the italicized words, imagine you were kissing your favourite person at the time!)

8   *Don't be worried that your accent is not perfect.*
Think how charming a French accent in English can sound. People don't want you to pretend to be someone you're not! An English accent when speaking French can be endearing to French people. A colleague learning Japanese was delighted to be told that her English accent when speaking Japanese was regarded as really cute!

9   *Tune in to the music.*
This is called 'intonation' in languages. It's the 'music' of the language. You may have noticed, for example, that Welsh people use English with considerably more 'song' than native English people? Think back to very young children as they start speaking – they seem to get the 'music' of their words right long before they get the words themselves grammatically correct. They often succeed in making themselves understood more through their 'music' than their words. You can do this too, now.

10 *Make it physical!*
Doing something involving your muscles, while learning a new idea, can help you retain and master the idea. Some people like running or swimming as an aid to their learning of the more complex ideas of a language. When the muscles are busy, the brain seems free to take in new ideas. Link your language learning with exercise. You can often use the rhythm of exercise to help your mind master the rhythm of using words in a new language.

While we're exercising, many of the everyday events that crowd our brains are temporarily put to the background, and it's quite easy to get our brains to concentrate on a chosen idea, perhaps the last ten new words you've just learned. In fact, when we're walking, swimming or even running, our brains are often highly retentive and inventive. Many people get their most useful ideas while on the move rather than sitting still. Let movement help your learning.

11 *Keep learning more words.*
Stick up post-it notes with new words on them – round your dressing-table mirror or shaving mirror. Stick them beside the kitchen sink, around your computer screen; wherever you spend time. Get to 'see' these new words.

12 *Put labels on things!*
Stick post-it notes on household objects, with their names in the language you're learning.

13 *Play language games.*
For example, make three sets of cards: The first one could be for pronouns (I, you, he, she, it, we, they, and so on – in the language you're learning); the second for verbs (regular and irregular); and the third for tenses (present, past, future).

Turn up a card from each pile, and test yourself as to how quickly you can speak the pronoun and verb in the correct tense. Verbs mean action. If you can master action in any language, you're well on your way to mastering the language.

14 *Listen without worrying.*
Think back to when you were first discovering your own language. How much of a news broadcast or weather forecast did you understand? Very little! But hearing the words gradually adds up to discovering the language. When you listen, don't panic about all the words that mean nothing to you – rather be pleased about the odd word here and there that *does* mean something to you.

15 *Watch and learn!*
When watching television broadcasts or videos in the language

you're learning, forget about the words, and practise getting the meaning by watching what you see. Let your mind capture the messages of facial expression. Let your ears capture the messages of tone of voice and emphasis. All of this is important in learning any language.

16 *Get your timing right!*
In all languages, there are some important words to do with time. In English, such words include 'immediately, now, today, tomorrow, yesterday, soon, just now, recently, next week, a long time

ago' and so on. Think of your own language – it's more important that you know *when* you are than *where* you are! Get to grips with these words – there aren't many of them in any language.

17 *Get your emphasis right!*
In all languages, there are words for 'never, definitely, always, often, sometimes, very' and so on. These words add conviction to your messages. Remind yourself how important words like these are in your own language. It's interesting to now and then tape-record yourself in informal conversation, then simply sit back listening to which words are the most important ones when you are getting a message across. Find out the equivalent words in the new language – they'll be just as useful there.

18 *Get your 'fillers' ready!*
In all languages, there are words which mean nothing in particular, but which give the speaker time to think. In English, these include: 'Ah, well, but...'; or 'Well this is indeed true, but...'; or, 'Of course I see what you're saying...'; and 'You know what I'm getting at?'. Corresponding words and phrases exist in all languages. The more you can use them, the more time you will have to think of what to say next.

19 *Learn to hesitate!*
In English, this is sometimes as clumsy as 'er'! It can become a bit more eloquent, such as in:
'Well, I see what you're saying' or, 'I know what you mean' or, 'I've been there myself' and so on. This sort of language gives us time to assemble our thoughts for what we're going to say next.

20 *Stay with the flow.*
When you're listening to a conversation in a new language, don't stop and think about the meaning of particular words. Stay with all the other information that is coming to you: tone of voice; emphasis; facial expression; passion; emotion; stress; conviction; and so on. In any language, this 'information' counts more than the words themselves. Think of the language of love, that (if anything) is the only universal language known by all of our species!

10

TIPS AND WRINKLES | on learning a new language

1 Erase bad memories such as if you had to learn hundreds of 'irregular verbs' at school. Knowing them probably would not have been very important anyway.

2 Don't try to learn all of the language – start with things you know you may need (food, travel, money, courtesy, greetings, and so on).

3 When you can, eat in a restaurant where the menu is in the language you're trying to learn.

4 Entertain someone from the country whose language you're learning – have them stay with you for a week if possible.

5 See if there are any evening classes in the language at a local college, and join in.

6 Go on holiday to wherever the language is spoken.

7 Find yourself a pen-friend in the country where the language is spoken (this is easier than you may think!).

8 Listen to tapes of the language at home, or in the car, or on your personal stereo.

9 Speak the language a lot – don't just read about it. Use a tape recorder now and then to hear yourself speaking it.

10 Listen to foreign radio broadcasts from the country concerned – or satellite television broadcasts if you have the chance – but don't expect to gather too much at first, just let your mind tune in over weeks and months.

Chapter **9**

Getting your act together

Getting a grip on your learning

In this chapter, we'll look at some ways to make sure that you can get full credit for things you've learnt. This includes being able to get good marks in written exams. Even when you're not going in for formal tests or exams, it's useful to use ways that help you know for yourself that your learning has been successful.

Playing to win

How can we tell when we've learnt something? How can we tell when we've learnt it really well? You may feel you know when you've learnt something well. Sometimes indeed we can tell all by ourselves that our learning has been successful. We can see the results, we can stand back and admire our achievements, and feel proud of ourselves.

It's not what we've learnt that shows, but what we can do with what we've learnt. We can't connect our brains up to a computer system, key in a few commands, and obtain a printout of everything in our minds. (If ever this becomes possible of course, think how much work it would save regarding tests or exams. But also think of everything you'd prefer not to be seen on the printout!)

But can other people tell? When we get down to it, we need other people to tell us when we've learnt something successfully. Their responses may take all sorts of forms:

- applause at our performance
- asking us to do things for them that they now know we can indeed do
- measurements of our performance

In this last chapter, we'll return to the business of showing other people how well we've learnt – and that includes any examiners who may mark any written exam papers we go in for.

The more we anticipate exactly what we're going to *do* to show that our learning has been successful, the better we can prepare to show our learning at its best.

Quiz on revision

We're going to look at ten possible ways to polish up your learning. You may use these ten processes if you're trying to do some serious revision. However, not all of them are very efficient. Your task is to award each of the ten processes a 'star rating' for how efficient and effective you think it could be. The scale is:

★★★   for really efficient and productive
★★   for fairly efficient and productive
★·   for not very efficient or productive

(Catch: there's *one* option that's worth ★★★★ – can you work out which it is?)

Enter your 'stars' beside each option, and then compare your scoring with the discussion which follows. We'll then go on to look at ways of making the most of the really useful processes – as well as the reasons why some of the others are not really so useful.

(When you've entered all your 'star-ratings', compare your choices with those in our discussion overleaf.)

	Star rating
1 Reading notes or books over and over again	
2 Writing bits out over and over again	
3 Listening to it over and over again	
4 Answering questions in writing	
5 Answering questions 'orally' i.e. speaking the answers	
6 Quizzing fellow learners, and being quizzed by them	
7 Writing essays	
8 Making essay plans	
9 Solving problems, doing calculations and sums, etc.	
10 Making summaries of your notes and books	

Response to quiz on revision

Here, at a glance, are the 'star ratings' that I would give each of these revision processes.

	Star rating
1 Reading notes or books over and over again	★
2 Writing bits out over and over again	★★
3 Listening to it over and over again	(★)
4 Answering questions in writing	★★
5 Answering questions 'orally' i.e. speaking the answers	★★★
6 Quizzing fellow learners, and being quizzed by them	★★★★
7 Writing essays	★
8 Making essay plans	★★★
9 Solving problems, doing calculations and sums, etc.	★★
10. Making summaries of your notes and books	★★★

Some of the 'star ratings' above can be argued about – they're meant to be food for thought rather than definite answers. In the discussion that follows, we'll look at some reasons for the 'high ratings', and 'low ratings' given above, and explore a bit more about the advantages and disadvantages of each of these ways of polishing up your learning.

Why some revision processes are better

You may well have been wondering why I gave the star ratings as I did in my response to the quiz. The reasons are indeed important, and in the discussion which follows, we'll explore more about each of these processes. In particular, it's useful to compare each of them to the main factors in the ways that we learn efficiently and effectively, as discussed first in Chapter 1 of this book.

1   *Reading notes or books over and over again*   ★
    This may seem the most obvious way to get a grip on your learning. In fact, it is quite useful at first; until you start to be familiar with what you're learning. Then, however, it becomes rather tedious. It becomes oh so possible to read a couple of pages three times, and not actually take anything in. Have you had the feeling? Do you remember looking at books and notes – maybe for hours – with nothing actually going in to your brain? So although it works a little, it does not get a high 'star rating' for efficiency or effectiveness. If we look at it in terms of our straightforward model of learning, we can soon see why, as follows:

    • *wanting to learn:* reading over and over again becomes really *boring* – it doesn't help us to want to learn;
    • *learning by doing:* reading isn't really 'doing'. Reading is too passive to be really useful as a learning process – unless we're *doing things* all the time as we read, such as writing down questions, making summaries, highlighting key points, and so on;
    • *getting feedback:* not much really – reading alone doesn't give us much information about how much we've actually learnt;
    • *'making sense', 'digesting':* here, reading is quite reasonable. The more often we read something, the greater our chance of making sense of it. But there are even better ways of making sense of things than just reading them over and over again.

Verdict: not much good really, not worth spending a lot of time doing this.

2   *Writing bits out over and over again*   ★★
    I've given this two stars – maybe one-and-a-half would be a better choice (so if you chose one star, that's fine too). It's not worth three, simply because it takes too long to keep doing it. It works

quite well as a means of polishing up your learning, but is too slow. Let's see how it relates to our model of learning:

- *wanting to learn:* again, writing over and over again becomes boring, and can damage the want to learn;
- *learning by doing:* here, we're fine. Writing words out is learning by *doing* in a way that reading hardly ever can be;
- *getting feedback:* we can indeed find out some information about how we're doing, by seeing how easily we can write without looking at the original. Not too interesting a way of getting feedback, however.
- *'making sense', 'digesting':* again, there's some mileage here. The fact that we have to slow down to write often gives our brains a little more time to make sense of what we're writing. However, there's always the danger that we just end up *copying*, and that does not do much for us in terms of learning.

Verdict: alright in limited amounts, but not too efficient, and can become boring.

3 *Listening to it over and over again* (★)

You may well have wondered why I put some brackets in the 'star rating' for this one? This is because 'learning by listening' varies a great deal from person to person, and from subject to subject. For example, classical musicians can become highly skilled at 'learning by listening', and may be able to write down music that they've heard, but not seen on paper. The same can apply to drama and poetry; hearing it over and over again can help us to remember it. But listening does not really work for maths, chemistry, sociology, cookery, woodwork, and all sorts of other subjects. Let's see how it links to our model of learning:

- *wanting to learn:* if we like listening, it obviously will help our want to learn. It depends really how much we enjoy listening to whatever it is we're trying to learn from.
- *learning by doing:* listening isn't exactly 'doing' normally. Most listening is relatively 'passive' and our thoughts can easily stray away from what we hear.
- *getting feedback:* no, we can't really get much feedback on how our learning is going just by listening. Actually, on second thoughts, we can, if we're really listening *actively,* for example,

singing along or playing along with what we hear when learning music

- *'making sense', 'digesting':* listening can be quite useful as a way of helping us to make sense of what we learn. If we're listening to speech, for example, we have the added advantage of tone of voice and emphasis to help us sort out what's really important, and what isn't.

Verdict: a variable one. If you find it works for you, keep on listening.

4   *Answering questions in writing*   ★★

I've only given this one two stars. Yet it is the way that much of our learning is tested. Exams usually measure people's ability to answer questions in writing. So it is a useful way of polishing up your learning, especially if you're preparing for a written exam. Let's see what sorts of learning are involved in practising answering questions in writing, as follows:

- *wanting to learn:* it can become a bit tedious to keep writing the answers to questions, but it can also help to develop confidence in ourselves that we can indeed do this when needed, for example, in exams. So in general, the want to learn is assisted by answering questions in writing.
- *learning by doing:* this is definitely learning by doing. No problems here.
- *getting feedback:* we can indeed get feedback, if we check through our written answers, and see how good they actually were. Or we can have someone else check through our answers, and give us feedback.
- *'making sense', 'digesting':* this too is catered for by answering questions in writing. The act of trying to express something in writing is often a way of 'getting our heads around it'.

Verdict: a good way to polish our learning really, but it can be a bit slow.

5   *Answering questions 'orally', i.e. speaking the answers*   ★★★

Ah, now we're talking (literally!). Three stars? Why is this better than writing the answers to questions? Mainly because it's a whole lot quicker. This means that we can get through more questions in a given time. This means we can cover a lot more ground. The learning processes involved are very similar to those in writing out answers to questions, as follows:

- *wanting to learn:* because we can cover a lot of ground this way, and because it's less tedious than writing everything down, 'speaking the answers' can help us to want to keep on doing it.
- *learning by doing:* it's just as much learning by *doing* as writing the answers – but even faster.
- *getting feedback:* actually, the feedback side of things isn't as good as writing out the answers, because we can't go back so thoroughly to check that we've answered the questions well (unless, of course, we do it on tape, or have someone else listening and giving us feedback).
- *'making sense', 'digesting':* 'speaking the answers' is actually very good when it comes to making sense of something. We soon find when we can't find the words we want, that there's a bit more 'making sense' still to be done.

Verdict: a really good way of polishing up learning. Do at least some practice in writing as well, though, if, in due course, you're preparing for written exams.

6   *Quizzing fellow learners, and being quizzed by them*   ★★★★
So, this was the 'catch' one. Four stars, no less! Why is this? Because it's so active. Let's look straightaway at how it links to learning:

- *wanting to learn:* it can be very stimulating to quiz fellow learners, and be quizzed by them. It's a social activity after all. It can be done almost anywhere, including your favourite pub. Say no more about helping the want to learn!
- *learning by doing:* there's no better kind of doing than answering questions, indeed asking them and judging the answers you get from your fellow learners.
- *getting feedback:* this is the real winner. You get a great deal of feedback finding out how your learning is going, as you compare yourself to your fellow learners. And the feedback is immediate – you don't have to wait for it. Don't forget that it's *good news* when you find out that you don't yet know the

answer to a question – it's far better than not knowing you didn't know.

- *'making sense', 'digesting':* again, a real winner. Talking something through with fellow learners is probably the best possible way of helping you to make sense of it. Whenever you explain something to them, it helps you get a better grip on it yourself. Whenever they explain things to you, the chances are that you can understand their explanations even better than the ones you may have had from books, teachers, or tutors.

Verdict: the best of the bunch. Do it a lot – and enjoy doing it.

7   *Writing essays*   ★

We're going back a step here. The only reason that anyone would try to learn something by writing essays, is if they're preparing for a written exam or test where they will be asked to do exactly this. In this case it's relevant – but why only one star? Mainly because it's *so* slow! Let's see what sorts of learning are involved:

- *wanting to learn:* not helped much. Writing essays is a rather tedious and solitary activity – unless you really enjoy writing essays. (I prefer writing books!)
- *learning by doing:* well, it is learning by doing – we can't deny this – but being so slow, there's not a lot of 'doing' per half-hour if you see what I mean.
- *getting feedback:* not much feedback, unless you go through each essay very carefully and assess it – or give it to someone who can assess it for you (in which case you have to wait for the feedback).
- *'making sense', 'digesting':* not bad actually, but the fact that writing essays helps us make sense of a subject is not good enough on its own, in the light of the other comments above.

Verdict: something to do now and then for practice, but not a sensible strategy to base a whole revision programme on.

8   *Making essay plans*   ★★★

What's an 'essay plan' you may have asked when you first saw this option in our quiz? And why is it good enough for three stars? I'd better explain. An essay plan is a 'map' of what the final essay will contain. It can be a diagram, a flowchart, or just a list of the main headings that will be turned into paragraphs if the whole essay is written out in full.

Making an essay plan involves all the real thinking that goes into writing a full essay; in a fraction of the time. It involves making all the decisions about what to include, and about what the best order to structure the essay will be. You can make half a dozen essay plans in the time it would take to write out one full essay. Let's see what the learning payoff is:

- *wanting to learn:* this is catered for quite well, as making essay plans is never really time-consuming, and you don't get bored or bogged down in detail.
- *learning by doing:* in its way, making essay plans is a good way of learning by doing, as you'll be practising all the decision-making and prioritizing that you will need if, for example, you're required eventually to write essays in exams.
- *getting feedback:* you *can* get feedback on your essay plans, but really you have to go looking for it; by comparing your essay plans to other people's, and discussing the similarities and differences.
- *'making sense', 'digesting':* since you do a lot of thinking and decision-making when making essay plans, you'll actually also do quite a lot of 'making sense' as you go.

Verdict: a good way of doing a lot of thinking in a short time – and good practice if you've got essays to write later in exams.

9 *Solving problems, doing calculations and sums, etc.*   ★★
This is particularly appropriate if you're preparing for the sort of test or exam where most of the questions will be quantitative, or problem-type. Perhaps it should be worth a bit more than two stars on our scoring system? Perhaps it would really earn that extra star if you did it with a few fellow-learners, and tested each other on your answers, and compared notes – gaining that extra degree of feedback.

- *wanting to learn:* since this sort of practice is really relevant (if you're studying the appropriate kind of topic), you'll at least feel you're doing something worthwhile by practising in this way – and this helps to keep up your want to learn.

- *learning by doing:* yes, definitely, no problems here.
- *getting feedback:* you *can* get feedback if you check carefully whether your answers or solutions are correct, or work with fellow-learners who can help you do this.
- *'making sense', 'digesting':* this too is taken care of. Solving problems and doing calculations are both processes which help you make sense of what you're learning.

Verdict: a good one, when you're learning the sort of subject that requires problem solving or calculation. Good practice if you're working towards exams of this sort.

10 *Making summaries of your notes and books* ★★★

Another three-star one. The main reason is that it's so active. Another important reason is that it gives you something you can use again and again – maybe instead of having to keep going back to your original notes and books. Let's see what sorts of learning are involved in making summaries:

- *wanting to learn:* this is catered for rather well, as every time you make a summary, you have something new that you did not have earlier. As your pile of summaries builds up, you can see the ground you've covered.
- *learning by doing:* making summaries has the very important 'learning by doing' aspect of decision-making. When you make summaries, you're always consciously deciding 'what is important?' and 'what isn't important enough to include in the summary?'
- *getting feedback:* by far the best way to gain feedback on your technique of making summaries is to compare and contrast the ones you make with those made by fellow learners. So you can indeed benefit from the feedback side of things, however, you really have to go looking for it.
- *'making sense', 'digesting':* making summaries is an excellent way of 'making sense' of what you have been learning. Deciding what is important is part of this 'making sense'.

Verdict: an excellent way to polish up on your learning, and a technique that gives you something useful for further polishing.

Going in for an exam?

In many ways, this is the way to prove to everyone that your learning has indeed been successful. But what do exams actually measure? Let's look at a few of the myths about exams – and some of the truths.

Exams measure what you know
Only partly true! There will be many questions that you know the answer to, which you will not be asked on a particular exam paper.

Exams measure what you don't know
Only partly true again. Exams measure what you don't know about the particular questions that happen to be asked on that occasion.

Exams measure how intelligent you are
Not really true at all. Some of the most intelligent people who ever lived were never good at exams (not least Albert Einstein, the man who first worked out how 'relativity' works).

Exams measure your ability to keep your cool
Yes, quite true. Adopting a calm, logical and planned approach to tackling any exam pays dividends in terms of the marks you can gain.

Exams measure your time management skills
Yes, indeed. If you've got five questions to answer in three hours, and only answer three, your maximum possible mark is going to be 60%. It's very important to make sure that you're marked out of 100% so pay particular attention to splitting the available time sensibly, so that you give each question a fair crack of the whip.

Exams measure your ability to answer exam questions
Yes, yes, yes! This is the one. The more practised you are at answering exam questions, the better you will do in exams. After all, it's just another of those skills that we learn by doing, practising and finding out about our mistakes. Make as many as possible of your mistakes well before the exam.

Exams measure how often you've practised answering exam questions
Definitely! Practice makes perfect.

Let's finish this chapter with some practical, straightforward tips on preparing for an exam, and particularly for the way you approach your tasks in the exam room.

Things to do just before your exam

- *Before the day of the exam*, find out exactly *where* the exam room is. This can save you from spending vital energy looking for the right room on the day. Also double-check exactly *when* each exam is. Timetables for exams sometimes change, so make sure that you've got the latest information.

- *Check the precise exam format.* For example is it, 'do any four questions' or, 'do Question 1, two from part B of the paper, and one from part C'?

- *Collect together your 'bits and pieces',* for example: pens, pencils, calculator – spare battery, rubber, correction fluid, highlighting pen, drawing instruments – so that on the day of the exam, you only have to pick up one box or folder, rather than looking for all the items.

- *Don't work too hard!* If you work all of the night before an exam you'll certainly be too tired to do the questions justice.

- When doing your final revision, *don't depress yourself* by finding out everything you still don't know. Concentrate on polishing-up on that which you already know, and think positive!

- *On the day of the exam, aim to get there early.* Make sure you'll still have plenty of time if the car won't start, or if the train doesn't run, or if you miss the bus. Being late for an exam – or even just thinking you may be late – uses up a lot of valuable mental energy. Spare yourself stress – be early.

- *On the day of the exam, try to avoid stressful situations.* Don't argue with your partner. Don't let yourself get angry. Don't let anyone make you feel hassled.

- Immediately before your exam, it's best to *avoid the cluster of people outside the exam room* asking each other questions. If you participate, you'll almost certainly get the *feeling* that everyone around you seems to know a lot more than you do.

- As the starting time draws near, *think of what you* can *do*, not what you can't do. Remember that it's quite easy to get the first half of the marks for each question anyway.

- *Keep things in perspective.* Remember that it is *only an exam* – and not the be all and end all of everything. You can't do more than simply give it your best shot.

Those first few minutes of your exam

- *Make absolutely sure* when you sit down at your desk that you have nothing with you that could possibly be seen as material for 'cheating'.

- *Check you're looking at the right exam paper!* Often, several exams are under way in the same room.

- *Do the 'administrative' bits and pieces* – putting your name or candidate number, date and time of the exam, etc. on the various forms and exam booklets on your desk. This routine activity can help you feel more relaxed.

- *Check and double-check the instructions on the paper.* How many questions? How much time? 'Two from Section A' etc.? Compulsory questions?

- *Work out a timetable for the exam*, based on how many questions you need to do (leaving fifteen minutes or so spare for checking, towards the end of the exam). *Jot down* 'target start times' for each of the questions you will do.

- *If you've no choice of questions*, you may then wish to start with your first question – or you may wish to work out first which question is the *best* one for you to start with.

- *If you have a choice to make, spend time making wise choices.* Read each question in turn, *slowly, calmly, and more than once.* Decide which questions are 'possible' – mark them ✔; which are 'bad' – mark them '✘'; and decide which are 'good' – mark them ✔✔.

- *Ignore the fact that people around you are scribbling!* Spending five – even ten – minutes reading questions carefully and making wise choices earns you more marks than the first half-page they've written.

- *Feel free to spend a few minutes jotting down key ideas or information.* This can save you worrying about losing ideas that came into your mind when you first read the questions.

- *Choose to start with a* good *question*. This gives yourself the feeling that you're making real headway but watch the timing; good questions tend to overrun. Be concise.

- *Read your first question one more time* – then get stuck in to it remembering the total time you should aim to spend on it. (First questions tend to run on if you're not careful as you'll probably know a lot about the topic concerned.)

Writing your exam answers

- *Keep – within reason – to your timetable.* You'll get far more marks for five reasonable answers than for one long, brilliant one.

- If your time for a question runs out *leave a gap and move on* to another question. You can always come back and add more later. Your first question tends to overrun – maybe because you know too much about it!

- *Keep re-reading the questions as you answer them.* This helps you avoid going off on tangents. More marks are lost in exams by candidates going off on tangents, than by candidates not knowing what the right answers are.

- *Do exactly what the question asks – no more, no less.* Don't waste time and energy writing down anything which the question doesn't require you to do.

- *If you get stuck – leave your planned timetable for the moment – and move on to another question that you feel more comfortable with.* You can avoid mental blanks by *not* trying to force your brain to recall information that is temporarily unavailable to you.

- *For essay-type questions, spend the first few minutes planning your answer.* This helps to make sure that the essay has a promising 'beginning', a coherent 'middle' and a convincing 'conclusion'.

- *For numerical or problem-type questions, make sure the examiners can see exactly how you reached your answers.* Show clearly each step you take. If something goes wrong, you can still get marks for all that the examiners can *see* is correct.

- *Try to keep your sentences short and simple.* Less can go wrong with short sentences – there's less chance of the examiners reading them the wrong way.

- *Help your examiners with their marking.* Make it easy for them to see where you've finished one question and started another. If they can find their way easily through your script, their generosity tends to increase.

- *Every now and then give yourself a minute off.* Give your brain a chance to sort itself out. Give your thoughts time to put themselves into a sensible pattern.

Near the end of your exam

- *Don't leave early.* If you walk out before time is up, the chances are that you'll remember something important that you could have added to your answers.

- *Stop answering the exam questions!* Even if you're still in the middle of a question, there are usually more marks to be gained by following the suggestions below during the last fifteen minutes or so, than by continuing trying to finish the question.

- *Read your script from beginning to end,* even though you won't feel like doing this. You'll be surprised how many marks you can still gain. As you read, *make corrections*; you'll notice that some of your work isn't quite as you intended it to be.

- *As you read, make additions* – when important ideas have filtered into your mind *since* the time you wrote your answers.

- *As you read, make adjustments,* to make the meaning of key sentences and paragraphs easier for the examiner to follow.

- *Make your intentions clear.* For example, if you happened to make a 'false start' at a question, show which questions the examiners should take into account.

- *Now go back to unfinished questions.* If, and only if, you've still got time left, it may be worth going back to any unfinished questions, and trying to finish them off, possibly in note-form if time is really short.

- *If you've still got time left, do a bit of tidying up.* Make it easy for the examiner to find where each question starts and finishes. Make headings, main points and conclusions stand out a little more.

- *Stay at your desk till time is up.* Even during the last minute, an idea may come back to you, which is worth an extra mark or two.

- *After you leave, avoid all temptations to talk about the exam.* The exam is now over. Post-mortems demoralize. If you talk to people, you are certain to find out something they did that you did not think of at the time – and things you did wrongly. Also, the people who say they did really badly tend to do very well!

Where will it all end?

This is nearly the end of this book. However, it's only the start really. Being more aware of how we learn is the key to a whole new meaning to life. All of life is learning and we're equipped not only to learn but to *think* about how we learn. Once we develop the habit of doing this as part of our everyday lives, even the humdrum events of routine at work or at home become more interesting.

Furthermore, we need constantly to reassure ourselves that there are no limits on what we can learn. True, we're all better at some things than at others, but too often we tend to accept the (untrue) suggestion that for one reason or another certain skills are beyond us.

Even life's most distressing experiences are *learning* experiences. They may not seem useful at the time, but we emerge from them wiser and stronger and more competent. To live is to learn. The oft-repeated saying 'I think, therefore I am' should perhaps have been 'I learn, therefore I am'.

Perhaps the world would be a better place if we all pinned to our clothing the same 'L-plates' that we stick to our cars if and when we learn to drive. We're all learners. If we accept that we're learners, and if other people value us for declaring ourselves to be learners, errors or mistakes don't matter nearly so much – everyone forgives a learner a lot!

At the game of living, there is no doubt that 'who learns, wins'.

Further reading

500 Tips for Students
Phil Race, Blackwell, 1992

The Good Study Guide
Andrew Northedge, The Open University, 1990
A very detailed guide for college students, including in-depth
guidance on writing essays and working with numbers

How to Win as a Part-time Student
Tom Bourner and Phil Race, Kogan Page, 1991
Written specially for people returning to college as part-time
mature students

Lingo: how to learn a language
Terry Doyle and Paul Meara, BBC Books, 1991
A very enjoyable and friendly guide to anyone learning languages

The Mind Map Book: radiant thinking
Tony Buzan, BBC Books, 1993
Especially useful for those with a strong visual side to their thinking
and memory

Successful Study: a practical way to get a degree
Edited by Matt Hector-Taylor and Marie Bonsall,
The Hallamshire Press, 1993
An enjoyable little book for college students, full of useful tips
(and cartoons)

The Unforgettable Memory Book
Nick Mirsky, BBC Books/Penguin Books, 1994
A wonderful book that helps one to be proud of one's memory!

Index